THE SAVVY PART-TIME PROFESSIONAL

*How to Land, Create, or Negotiate the
Part-Time Job of Your Dreams*

Lynn Berger, MA, EdM

D1364195

CAPITAL SAVVY SERIES

CAPITAL
BOOKS, INC.
Sterling, Virginia

Capital Books, Inc.
P.O. Box 605
Herndon, Virginia 20172-0605

ISBN 10: 1-933102-18-7 (alk.paper)
ISBN 13: 978-1-933102-18-4

Library of Congress Cataloging-in-Publication Data
Berger, Lynn.
  The savvy part-time professional : how to land, create, or negotiate the part-time job of your dreams / Lynn Berger.
      p. cm. — (Capital savvy series)
  ISBN 1-933102-18-7 (alk. paper)
  1. Part-time employment. 2. Professional employees. I. Title. II. Series.

HD5110.B47 2006
650.14—dc22

2006013518

Printed in the United States of America on acid-free paper that meets the American National Standards Institute Z39-48 Standard.

First Edition

10 9 8 7 6 5 4 3 2 1

To my husband Dan for your endless support and encouragement and son Fred for your mirthful spirit and wonderful sense of humor.

ACKNOWLEDGMENTS

First, I want to thank Amy Fries and Kathleen Hughes for giving me the opportunity to write *The Savvy Part-Time Professional.* The project would not have been the same without assistance from Ming-yi (Grace) Gu—your hard work, enthusiasm, and dedication were greatly appreciated. I also want to thank Barbara Stern for all her help and support. I conducted many interviews for this book with colleagues, past clients, and friends within my community, and everyone asked was very willing to assist me. Last, I need and want to thank all the individuals (clients) I have worked with throughout the years. Many of your stories and challenges encountered are woven throughout the book.

NOTE: The Web site addresses listed in this book are all current at the time of publication. As we all know, however, Web sites come and go. If some are no longer in existence when you pick up this book—my apologies. I worked hard to find the best resources. However, the resources listed in this book are provided for information purposes only; a listing does not imply an endorsement.

CONTENTS

PREFACE

love my work. I've been a career counselor and professional coach for sixteen years, and my mission is to help each individual achieve his or her goals. To do that, I believe each person needs to look carefully at his or her life and to summon the courage to reevaluate decisions and choices when necessary.

Why? Because as we grow, our values change. For example, when we become parents, the office is no longer our first priority. Or after we've devoted twenty years to a career and accumulated more possessions than we want, we may look around and ask: What else is there in life? Or when we become empty nesters or face retirement, we must reconsider where we devote our energies. At these times, to attain harmony, we need to decide what's most important to us in our personal and professional lives: work, family, creating art, starting a business, exploring our spirituality or the world around us, or all of these.

As we progress in our careers and lives, we begin to understand what truly motivates us and how we can make the best choices. For many of you, this may include the option of part-time work. Why not try to have it all—work and a life? But deciding where your priorities are at a particular moment is not an easy task. In fact, it's tough. That's why I wrote this book. I use my experience to help you determine whether you can make a part-time profession and a full-time LIFE work for you.

If you've picked up this book to see if part-time work might suit you, you've already shown that you have the courage and willingness to believe you could succeed in reshaping your career much more to your liking. I believe taking risks is about making good choices. This book will help you evaluate risks and help you understand how to make the best decisions that will enhance the quality of your life for many years.

I also give you insight into part-time work options and answer the questions of how and where to find fulfilling part-time work as well as how to negotiate a part-time position with your present employer. As we all know, there are many fantastic resources on the Internet, but it can take hours, days, even months of searching. I like to think that I've done the research for you, so you have all the information or links to information in one handy guide. Depending on your circumstances, you probably won't feel the need to read the entire book; however, you might find it interesting to read about other Savvy Part-Time Professionals to gain an additional perspective. I use many real-life examples of people engaged in part-time work. Though they're all real people, to protect their privacy, I chose to use fictitious names.

The key point to remember as you read and complete the exercises is to keep in mind that your goal is to make your life richer and fuller—whatever that means for you. I tell my clients to "go for what you want." Try to make your life as meaningful and fulfilling as possible. Base your decisions and actions on your individual tastes, desires, skills, and values. Take appropriate risks and attempt to live with no regrets.

Now I can't say you'll get everything you want. Maybe you'll get it all, or maybe you'll get the greatest part and compromise on lesser details. That's all right. The main thing is—you gain by trying. When you search for what you want and ask for what you want, you gain confidence. If you apply the suggestions in this book with commitment and patience, you're very likely to gain a fulfillment and happiness you never would have found without risking change.

If you don't search and you don't ask, you already know the answer. Just try to imagine yourself sitting someplace several years from now, reflecting on your life and career. Let's make sure you don't have any regrets and that you make the most of your life.

—Lynn Berger, MA, EdM, Career Counselor and Coach

CHAPTER 1

Making the Case for Part-Time Work

I f you've picked up this book, chances are you're already drawn to the idea of working part-time. Or maybe you're intrigued but don't know where to start, or you haven't considered all the arguments. Most good decisions in life take some research. The more you know, the better the choice you'll make.

In this chapter, I help you determine if part-time work is the right personal choice for you. But first, let me make the case for part-time work in general.

To start, let's ask: what is part-time work? The word used to have a negative connotation. Part-time work was for someone who couldn't get a "real" job. Today, many people approach this option with more imagination, and part-time work isn't something they settle for but something they choose. Sometimes that choice is financial—they need the extra money. Sometimes working part-time is about fulfillment and creativity or simply getting out into the world.

Part-time also used to be seen as strictly hourly wage, but more and more professionals are choosing this as a career track. More than thirty-two million U.S. employees work part-time, and a growing number of those part-timers are managers and professionals (*Employment and Earnings*, Bureau Publication, Bureau of Labor Statistics. 2003, 2005.)

How you define part-time work is personal. If you're used to working sixty hours a week, then forty hours a week may seem like part-time to you. It also helps to think of part-time as a fluid option that may work better during some phases of your life than others. For example, part-time work may be a good fit when you're a new parent, going back to school, or exploring a passion. But it may be impossible when two college tuition payments are due, and you're the sole family provider. What I help you do in this book is to reevaluate your needs, priorities, and options as you move through life stages with the goal of answering the question: Am I living my life to the fullest?

"Occupation Is Essential," But So Is Leisure

The famous writer Virginia Woolf once said, "Occupation is essential," meaning that people need a purpose in life and constructive activities, whether paid or unpaid (homemaking, parenting, volunteering). It's equally true, however, that all work and no play makes Jack a dull boy—or, worse yet, a bad parent or lousy companion. A part-time position allows many people to have the best of both worlds: time to work and time to take breaks to satisfy other needs and desires.

With so much to do and so little time, why not consider part-time work? How much money do you really need? If you're happy, you'll probably need less. Think about the possibility of pursuing more activities that you actually enjoy. The possibilities are endless. By working part-time, you could have time for friends and family, travel, arts and crafts, exercise, philanthropic work, and spiritual growth, to name a few.

Remember, life is an adventure if you're open to it. Try to have as many positive experiences as possible.

Workaholic Lifestyle

How many of us have time to think, reflect, play, or do nothing? Very few. This is a sad fact, since a lot of life is about thinking, reflecting, playing, or just doing nothing. Many times, a person goes through a period of boredom before he or she comes up with a wonderful idea or dares to pursue an extraordinary adventure. Since few people have downtime any more, there's not a lot of room or time for this to happen.

Today, the majority of Americans have very few hours of leisure after their jobs and household chores. This is getting worse as a result of society's increasing debt and excessive spending. We work longer to earn money to purchase things we probably don't need and, in some cases, don't even want. As a result of being stuck on the money merry-go-round, many people have become addicted to a workaholic lifestyle. They work harder and harder to pay off debt, but they don't seem to get any happier in the process. Learning to think about what you really need, what you consume, and how you manage your debt will increase your options for change. I discuss these financial challenges and options and how to determine if you can afford a part-time profession more in chapter 2.

Millions of Americans Are Overworked, Overscheduled, and Just Plain Stressed Out

It seems that today many people would trade time for money or other benefits. When I ask many of my clients what they want more of in life, it's usually time for themselves, family, friends, and creative pursuits. Our workaholic tendencies might appear to make us profitable (if we ignore our debt), but such tendencies also have a serious downside. According to a report by the Families and Work Institute, "The majority of employed Americans feel deprived of time." As a result, we lack balance.

According to a Families and Work Institute study, "When Work Works," "67% of employed parents say they don't have enough time with their children; 63% of married employees don't have enough time with their spouses, up from 50% in 1992; and in 2002, the only year in which the question was asked, 55% of all employees say they don't have enough time for themselves."

Other findings from the Families and Work Institute study include:

- One in three American employees feels chronically over-worked.
- Some time in the past month, 54 percent of American employees have felt overwhelmed by how much work they had to complete.
- Seventy-nine percent of employees had access to paid vacations in 2004, *but* more than one-third of employees (36 percent) had not planned to take their full vacation.
- On average, American workers take 14.6 vacation days annually. However, most employees take short vacations, with 37 percent taking fewer than seven days. Only 14 percent of employees take vacations of two weeks' duration or longer.
- Among employees who take one to three days off (including weekends), 68 percent return feeling relaxed, compared with 85 percent who feel relaxed after taking seven or more days (including weekends).
- Only 8 percent of employees who are not overworked experience symptoms of clinical depression, compared with 21 percent of those who are highly overworked.

Effects of Overwork on Your Health

I was at a meeting recently sitting beside a gentleman in his mid-fifties, and I asked him how he was. He said he was terrific—he'd just retired. I was stunned since he was in good health, very successful, and seemed happy with his work. He told me he'd decided to retire because he didn't want to die at his desk like his father did. He wanted to enjoy himself and reap the benefits of his hard work.

The comment about his father dying at his desk may be an exaggeration, but it isn't far off the mark. The effects of overwork can be devastating. Excessive stress can kill, symptoms of stress range from headaches to major diseases, and too much stress can disrupt your eating and sleeping patterns and hurt your relationships.

Take control before it's too late. There are usually subtle warning signs and messages; the key is to pay attention to them. If you're beginning to have back pain—take it easy. Ask yourself why and how it occurred. You can and should do the same with other ailments. Be prepared by developing effective coping methods and techniques to use when the stress in your life becomes too much. I refer to it as your personal toolbox; attempt to fix it before it falls apart. For some it might be taking a walk; for others sitting quietly, calling a friend, going to the gym, drawing a picture, or listening to music. There are many simple stress-reducing activities; the trick is to find the ones that work for you.

Obviously, if you are overworked and cannot maintain the pace you've set, you need to make some adjustments. Finding the right balance in life should be your goal, and in that vein, you should explore the option of part-time work.

Questions That Can Help You Determine If You're "Burned Out"

The answers to some of the following questions can be very revealing, and you should take them seriously if you want to enhance the quality of your professional and personal life.

- Has your work felt too demanding in the last few months? Has it interfered with your personal life?
- Do you have enough downtime to think about your responsibilities and priorities?
- Are you able to enjoy your time away from the office?
- How often do you find yourself confused or unfocused even when your job is clearly defined?
- During your vacations, do you still call your office, and do your co-workers call you?
- Do your bosses, supervisors, customers, or clients interrupt your home life?

Part-Time and Other Flexible Work Options Are Good for Business

Nothing works better for an employer than a happy and contented employee. People appreciate flexibility and being treated with respect, especially when it comes to recognizing their personal responsibilities and needs. Offering creative work/life balance opportunities is also a way for smaller companies to compete with the "big benefits" of larger, established corporations.

Numerous studies highlight the benefits to the employer or company of providing flexible work options. For example, employees with flextime opportunities:

- remain longer in their positions;
- exhibit increased motivation and willingness to do the job;
- report enhanced job satisfaction;
- help out more in times of employer need; and
- demonstrate heightened creativity on the job and evidence less stress.

Parents aren't the only ones who want more flexibility. According to the Families and Work Institute:

- Twenty-four percent of women and 13 percent of men who are full-timers would prefer to work part-time.
- Fifty-seven percent of older workers would also like to remain in the workforce working part-time. This preference for reduced hours is expected to become increasingly important as the workforce ages.
- Flexibility is also important to younger workers. Only 13 percent of women under forty-five who don't have children, but do plan to have them someday, think they'll return to work as soon as possible. That means plenty of professional women are planning to reduce their work hours at some point.
- The majority of men (68 percent) and the majority of

nonparents (70 percent) use flextime when they have it.

- In addition to the Families and Work Institute report, the *Wall Street Journal* reported on a study that concluded that "60% of workers of all ages rate time and flexibility as a very important factor in retention."

Part-Time Work Will Not Stifle Your Career

Many people think that if they go part-time, they'll miss out on promotions and effectively end their professional growth. In some situations, part-time professional jobs can become a dead end—if you let them. But there's been a sea change in corporations regarding flextime over the last decade, and the trend promises to continue—all of which is good news for the part-time professional.

The work world is changing as the population ages and as employees demand a better work/life balance. Corporations are beginning to realize that they need to get creative with flexibility if they want to hold on to their top-level employees. With vision and courage, you can learn to capitalize on the changes.

A 2005 Families and Work Institute study funded by the Alfred P. Sloan Foundation found that professionals who chose to work fewer hours did not derail their careers. In fact, study researcher Mary Dean Lee of McGill University calls part-time work the "new career track" and is quoted in *Newswise* as saying, "Even for demanding corporate jobs, part-time work is a viable path to career success and a fulfilling personal and family life."

Professor Lee also said in various interviews regarding the study that although the part-time trend was started by women in the 1990s, men are showing an interest in part-time careers as well.

Among the study's highlights:

- Nearly half of study participants were still working reduced hours six years after the end of the study—most of them

for large organizations and some were self-employed.
- On average, participants were earning salaries equivalent to those of full-time workers.
- More than half of those who continued part-time received one or more promotions.
- Nearly all part-timers received regular salary increases.
- Those who did switch back to full-time did so reluctantly because they were the main providers in their family.

(To see the entire study, "Crafting Lives that Work: A Six-Year Retrospective on Reduced-Load Work in the Careers and Lives of Professionals and Managers," go to http://web.manage ment.mcgill.ca/reports/md_lee/2005report1.pdf.)

The Need to Restructure (or Rethink) Work

AN ECONOMIC REALITY

As baby boomers exit the labor force, there will be a lack of talented leadership, mentors, and employees. To attract and keep a skilled and educated workforce, companies will need to expand flextime and part-time opportunities. In addition, aging baby boomers will need to work (to finance a longer life span and depend less on Social Security) and will want to work to remain stimulated, happy, and active. I discuss this subject extensively in chapter 8.

Corporations also can't afford to lose highly educated and talented women (and men) who feel the need to take time off to parent or take care of elderly relatives.

A LIFESTYLE CHOICE

Many individuals who have or had high-powered jobs or ran companies feel forced to change direction because of the excessive and unreasonable demands made on them. For example, journalist Matt Miller recently explored the need to redesign our concept of work in an article in the *New York Times*, titled "Listen to My Wife." In the article, Miller argues that we need to change the way jobs are structured. For example, his wife used to run a company, but she stopped working full-time to be a mom. She now works part-time at a job that Miller feels uses only a fraction of her skills. "Many of society's most talented people feel they have to sacrifice the meaningful relationships every human craves as the price of exercising their talent." According to him, talented people are throwing up their hands and "opting-out" after deciding their professional success isn't worth the price.

Miller and his wife believe the answer is to reengineer the jobs and the corporate culture that sustains them and that both men and women need to join in this. Miller goes on to say, "A broader drive to redesign work will take a union-style consciousness that makes it safe for men who secretly want balance to say so."

The Families and Work Institute cites other trends that bode well for part-time professionals:

- The Center for Women's Business research estimates that women-owned firms are "growing at close to twice the rate of all privately held firms." And women presumably are more attuned to the needs of work/life balance.
- "Twenty-six percent of the current wage and salaried workforce plans to be self-employed or have their own business in the future."

Loss of Female Talent

Despite moves in the right direction, only 8 percent of top corporate officials at Fortune 500 companies are women, according to "The Corporate Gender Gap," in *The Week* magazine. This is extremely low given that women now comprise approximately 50 percent of the workforce. Something is not letting them rise to the highest levels. Many women are starting at the same point as men, but by the time they reach age thirty and forty, many of them have dropped out. Why? The primary career-building years are the ones that match up with childbearing and childrearing years. Many women feel they can't have high-powered corporate careers and still enjoy a balanced family life.

As a result, many women who can afford it, opt out of the workplace. A recent survey by the research and advocacy organization, Catalyst (www.catalystwomen.org) found that one in three women with MBAs was not working full-time. For men, that ratio is one in twenty.

Similar studies illuminate how highly capable, resourceful women become corporate dropouts. Usually a breaking point occurs when business demands preclude them from attending important family events. At some point, the compromise seems too much. As a result, hundreds of thousands are dropping out. According to sociologist Arlie Hochschild, many corporate women who leave would prefer to keep working if they could manage it. As it is, many women decide to work from home or start their own business in lieu of working for high-pressure corporate America.

The resulting loss to corporate America is great. The good news is that some progress is being made, and companies are slowly beginning to realize they must become more creative if they want to retain talented employees. Imagine how wonderful it would be if more individuals could be working part-time for an extended period and be welcomed back full-time later. This would certainly reduce the corporate gender gap and allow companies to keep the talent they've nurtured.

Fathers Need Flexibility, Too

Women aren't the only parents who need and want part-time work. Men need flexibility in their lives as well. How often do you see fathers at daytime school events? Throughout my years of attending programs with my son, there were very few times when a father was present. Even though dads are more involved in parenting than ever before, most of them are weekend dads. That's despite a Families and Work Institute study that reveals that a significant portion of men would love to have flexible work arrangements but would not dare ask in view of society's expectations. For example, a Catalyst study found that both men and women feel it's less socially acceptable for a man to ask for a flexible work arrangement than it is for a woman.

Consulting, working from home, and starting a business are all as viable for men as they are for women. The biggest challenge for men seems to be getting over the cultural stigma associated with gender and work. Many believe that when both genders start to use part-time arrangements, as they are beginning to do, the situation will become commonplace and acceptable.

Professional Part-Time Opportunities Are Growing

Part-time used to be seen as strictly a low-wage, low-status proposition, but more and more creative, ambitious people are changing that perception. As you see from the "real-life examples" throughout this book, professionals—lawyers, sales managers, librarians, teachers, entrepreneurs—are finding ways to carve out reduced schedules for themselves. According to the Bureau of Labor Statistics, approximately 20 percent of "professionals" worked part-time in 2004 (www.pardc.org/UpToPAR).

The Project for Attorney Retention (www.pardc.org) studies part-time work at law firms and develops "best practices recommendations." According to the organization's Web site, "Usage of part-time programs by attorneys is slowly rising."

Working Like a Slave Will Not Save You from the Ax

It's harsh, but true. We've experienced a major structural change in labor markets in the last twenty years. We have a new definition of job security—there is none. It's no longer lifetime employment like it was thirty years ago. The message is: if you don't perform, you're dispensable. This attitude leads people to believe that they must work twice as hard and long to prove their value to their employer. However, such dedication is no longer a guarantee of anything. Many individuals who have been laid off or downsized now see that giving up all their leisure time for the sake of their job didn't work. I know many people who gave their hard efforts to corporations and were let go for reasons that had nothing to do with them personally. Many of those evenings at the office went unnoticed when companies were facing layoffs.

People need to ask themselves how much energy and effort they should expend in working. What's the right balance? Are they taking care of their own needs as well as their employers'? Making a conscious decision about work/life balance can soften the blow if circumstances change and your position is eliminated.

One result of the end of job security is the need for a much more flexible labor force, one that can deal with change. A rapidly changing workplace means more layoffs and company restructuring. You can mitigate the risk of finding yourself suddenly unemployed by having two or more part-time jobs instead of one full-time job. This way "all your eggs aren't in one basket"—an old but wise saying and one you should keep in mind.

PORTFOLIO CAREERS

In a "portfolio career," a person has more than one job. Ideally, these multiple jobs won't run you ragged, but will give you flexibility in the workplace. Having a portfolio career, if you manage it correctly, can minimize your risk in a changing market and make you better able to deal with change or termination, if it should occur.

The first time I was introduced to portfolio careers was in Charles Handy's classic book, *The Age of Reason*. Since its publication, the notion of portfolio careers has grown in popularity, which is exactly what he predicted.

Portfolio careers remain a trend of the future. As management guru Peter Drucker states, "Corporations once built to last like pyramids are now more like tents...you can't design your life around a temporary structure."

Other Countries Make It Work; We Can, Too

Other countries take more time off—why not the United States? A lot of it is attitude. We believe that hours worked equals a higher quality of work, but that isn't always the case. The notion of working smarter, not longer needs to be introduced more into our society and work ethic. A friend of mine who has lived in many countries throughout the world once stated very simply, everyone works too hard here.

The culture of long hours at work is not universal. According to an article available on the Take Back Your Time Web site (www.timeday.org), "On average, Americans work nearly nine full weeks (350 hours) longer per year than our peers in Western Europe. In addition, working Americans average a little over two weeks of pure vacation per year, while Europeans average five to six weeks."

It is difficult to relax totally in one or two weeks, and the lack of leisure time can contribute to an unbalanced life. The Europeans I talk to relish their time off. They spend more time visiting family, relaxing, and taking care of their personal business than Americans do. This clearly contributes to their satisfaction and their increased productivity and efficiency.

Let me cite a specific example. Recently I met with a gentleman who left the United States for an assignment in London. He spent three and a half years there and enjoyed it tremendously. In New York, according to him, he worked like a "dog." He said he never had a true day off, and when he was on vacation, he still felt compelled to check in with the office. In England, he said, they are much more reasonable. Their expectations are different. When a senior partner in an accounting firm takes a holiday—they leave the work to a junior employee. Only in a dire emergency is the individual told to contact the partner. All of this man's experience in the United States has been totally different. When a senior partner in his U.S. firm is on vacation, the company is still in touch with him, often asking him to work. As he looks around and sees the life he will have to live as a senior partner in the United States, he says, "I don't want this." At this point, he is examining his options for a new career or a new position within his present company. But in all likelihood, the firm will probably end up losing an intelligent, hard-working young man due to its unreasonable expectations.

Here are some examples of better balance in other countries:

- "In European countries, not only are the hours that can be worked regulated and limited, but lengthy holidays are specified by law with stipulations about maternity and even paternity leave. In August, many factories and offices are closed. The foreign tourist in Paris during that time frequently finds restaurants and shops shut for 'les vacances.' Government offices maintain only skeleton staffs" (*Japan Times*.)
- "In Spain and Italy, especially but not solely during summer months, offices and shops are generally shut from 1 p.m. to 5 p.m. for the siesta" ("Commitment to Fewer Hours: Balancing Work with Other Ways of Life," *Japan Times*).
- Adults in Germany work 36.7 hours per week on average and have up to six weeks of annual leave. This means they have almost 2,500 hours of free time each year that they can use for relaxing as well as a wide range of activities such as travel, culture, entertainment, etc. (http://www.tatsachen-ueber-deutschland.de/499.0.html).
- Ireland passed legislation protecting the rights of part-time workers in 2001, ensuring among other things that part-time employees can't be treated "in a less favorable manner than a comparable full-time employee."
- In the United Kingdom, the law guarantees proportional pay and benefits for part-time workers.

Consider this information from the Harvard-based Project on Global Working Families:

- Some ninety-six countries "in all geographic regions and at all economic levels mandate paid annual leave. The U.S. does not require employers to provide paid annual leave."
- "At least 98 countries require employers to provide a mandatory day of rest: a period of at least 24 hours off each week. The U.S. does not guarantee workers this weekly break."
- "At least 84 countries have laws that fix the maximum length of the work week. The U.S. does not have a maximum length of the work week or a limit on mandatory overtime per week."

There are movements in the United States to bring more balance to our lives. Organizations such as Take Back Your Time and the Families and Work Institute strive to find the right mix between work and life. Unions in the United States have also been actively lobbying for a shorter work week. But, ultimately, it's up to each of us individually to assess our lives and take the steps necessary to reclaim our time.

Others Did It, So Can You

When a person gets caught up in working around the clock in true workaholic style, he or she loses sight of the fact that there is another way to work and live. However, once people get a taste of other possibilities, they begin to see the options for change.

For example, a client of mine who worked at a very highly regarded consulting firm observed this fact when she was home one day from work due to personal business and realized not everyone worked the same way she did. She saw that people in her building were receiving Federal Express packages during the day. It occurred to her that although they might be working, it certainly wasn't in the style to which she was accustomed.

She was becoming increasingly dissatisfied with her work and life, which spurred her to consider other options. A glimpse of what life could be like inspired her, and she decided to go back to school to study psychology and work in the field in a private practice.

Here are some other examples of people who made it work. I hope they will inspire you or at least open you to the possibilities: The names of the individuals are fictitious, their stories are not.

- Sam had an interest in photography and wanted to have time to see the places in the world he wanted to photograph. He left his full-time, high-pressure work as a public relations executive to work on his own. It was scary and frightening at first, but over time he realized he had made the right decision.
- Mary wanted to write children's books, so she left her job in the financial world. She took writing classes, met other writers, attended conferences, and began to write a children's book.
- Bruce wanted to write plays. To do this, he left his full-time job as a lawyer in the entertainment industry and took on various part-time jobs in his area of interest.
- Jane wanted to live without constant stress and anxiety and asked for a four-day work arrangement. Because she was so highly valued, the company agreed, and now she has a day during the week to pursue her writing and other creative endeavors.
- Sara had a high-pressure job in marketing that required traveling all over the world and meeting with many high-powered executives. She had two children and decided to work part-time at the same company. She was pleased with her decision as it allowed her to spend time with her kids. As it turned out, she was highly respected at the company for choosing to do what she did.
- When Patrick retired from his position as a small-business

owner he realized that he wasn't ready for that world yet. When a pizzeria became available for rent, he decided to seize the opportunity of having his own establishment. Since his wife still worked full-time, he was lonely at home. Now he enjoys the camaraderie and structure his work provides.

Still think part-time options are impossible? Not for these people. They made it happen, and so can you. Use their stories for inspiration. For all of them, it took time, patience, persistence, and understanding their priorities and needs.

Resources

- Ellen Galinsky, James T. Bond, and E. Jeffrey Hill, *When Work Works: A Status Report on Workplace Flexibility* (New York: Families and Work Institute, 2002) available online at www.familiesandwork.org
- Institute for Women's Policy Research, www.iwpr.org
- The Project on Global Working Families, http://www.hsph. harvard.edu/globalworkingfamilies/
- Take Back Your Time, www.timeday.org

CHAPTER 2

Is Part-Time Right for You?

F ace it. All of us would like to work less, but can we make it happen? Can we make it work financially? Do we have the imagination and the tolerance for risk that it takes to reenvision our lives? We explore these issues in this chapter.

In this chapter, I show you how to identify your values, interests, and skills to make a successful career transition. After that, I discuss the part-time options available. For example, do you currently have a job that's adaptable to part-time, or do you need to find or create a new one? Do you want to reduce your hours at work drastically, or are you simply looking for more flexibility via telecommuting, four-day work weeks, or flextime?

As you'll discover, there are many ways to work less and live more.

Can You Afford to Go Part-Time?

The optimal time to reassess your financial situation and determine your basic needs and expectations regarding compensation is when you're considering a career transition. This sounds obvious, but quite a few people never take the time to compare how much money they need to live the life they want with how much they need to finance that life. That's usually because they've put off thinking about the life they want. Instead, they've walked blindly down the road: accepting the first job they were offered, staying at a job they despised due to fear of change, or living in an expensive McMansion because that's what everyone else was doing.

I'll talk more about this later—how to figure out what you truly value in life and how to go after it. But first, you need to figure out the economics of going part-time, because if you can't make that work, then you're setting yourself up for failure.

How much money do you need to live? Go through this process on several levels. First, how much money do you need to pay your bills? Then how much do you need to pay bills and have some left to save for the future? After saving for the future, how much do you have left for your leisure activities?

Create a weekly and monthly budget by analyzing your income and spending habits. This is the important part: Ask yourself if what you're spending money on coincides with your values (I discuss how to identify your values in chapter 3).

Many people have no idea where they spend their money and are astonished at the end of the month to find that they spend more than they earn. If you begin to identify unnecessary expenses, perhaps you can cut down on hours at work and still meet your financial obligations.

You don't want to procrastinate when it comes to your personal finances. Many people don't like to deal with financial issues, but ignoring them won't help. Falling into debt or mindlessly earning and spending have subtle and not so subtle ways of ruining your life. One day you might wake up and ask, "Where did my life go?"

So, I highly recommend that you begin taking control of your time and how you spend your hard-earned dollars. I also recommend that you meet with a qualified financial adviser to help you assess your fiscal situation. In addition, many books, articles, and software programs are geared specifically to the topic of money management.

To get started with your budget, ask yourself the following questions:

- How much total or combined income do you have coming in?
- How much do you have after taxes?
- What are your biggest expenses? House? Car? Vacations? Child care? Can those be modified in any way? Remember, working less should save you on child care. How about trading in your car for a more affordable model? Can you lower your mortgage? (Where you live is huge. See chapter 9, Work/Life Balance, for more information).
- How much do you spend on daily living expenses? Take a hard look at such expenses as gasoline, dining out, wardrobe—these are places where you can save a considerable amount of money if you cut back on time at the office.
- What expenses are negotiable? In other words, would you trade take-out food four times a week and expensive lunches for a job that made you happier?
- What do you estimate you could earn if you job share or switch to part-time? (See chapter 4 for links to salary information.)
- Based on the above, how does a job share or part-time situation fit with your economic needs?

Further Resource

- A collaboration between the Community Action Partnership and the National Endowment for Financial Education, www.managingmymoney.com has many worksheets and tips on money management

Ten Ways to Manage Financial Stress

More and more people are striking out on their own in entrepreneurial ventures or choosing to work part-time—some for the flexibility of being their own boss and some for the opportunity to work at home and be closer to their family, hobbies, nature, or whatever it is they love. This can be an exhilarating and scary venture. Here are the top ten ways to manage the financial stresses you encounter if you choose to work part-time.

1. I know it's hard, but don't focus on increasing revenue initially—reduce costs. At first, this probably won't feel natural or intuitive.

2. If working at home, recognize that working outside the home is expensive. For example, you'll need less formal clothing, so dry cleaning expenses will automatically be lower. You can prepare and eat lunches at home. Finally, with the price of gas, most people will save a bundle on commuting expenses.

3. The average household spends approximately 10 to 25 percent of its income on unnecessary items. It's also true that, due to a lack of organization and resourcefulness, the average family wastes 5 to 10 percent of its revenue. Don't spend mindlessly; give it serious thought. Convert the cost of the desired object to the time spent at work—"This cappuccino maker is equivalent to a day's work." Is it worth the trade? Maybe—if coffee is a pleasure that will bring you more than instant gratification. Or is it going to end up in the basement after a couple of months? Don't buy unnecessary items in the first place, but if you do, rectify the mistake by selling or returning them.

4. Build satisfaction in other areas of your life. Instead of "getting" more objects, get more love, friends, time, pleasure, knowledge, energy, and space in your life.

5. If you think working part-time leaves you short on money, figure out what the gap is—in other words, how much additional money beyond your part-time position will you need to cover expenses, then start exploring additional income streams. This may include anything for which you have an interest, skill, or passion. For example, you could bridge your expense gap by tutoring a couple of hours a week, consulting, or creating a new product or service. You could also sell on eBay, rent a room, or walk dogs at lunchtime. Don't limit your imagination.

6. Clean out your closets. Getting rid of clutter is a mental boost. You can sell items that have outlived their usefulness or you can donate them; save the receipt for a tax deduction.
7. Rent, don't buy. For example, rent specialized home tools instead of buying them; rent DVDs instead of buying them.
8. Work out shared babysitting arrangements with neighbors and friends. In addition, consider carpooling for transporting your children to their many activities.
9. Barter services with friends, neighbors, and others in the community. For example, an accountant may want to barter services with an electrician.
10. Change your habits. Instead of shopping at the mall, go to the park or take a walk. The added bonus will be a healthier lifestyle.

Many of these suggestions require you to reevaluate your lifestyle choices. Finding a better work/life balance is key for those deciding to go part-time. In chapter 9, I also discuss how relocating to a lower-cost community can help you gain the freedom you desire. Big life changes require imagination, vision, and courage. Start thinking about them!

Benefits

When considering part-time work, you need to take a hard look at benefits. Will you be able to maintain benefits such as health insurance and retirement accounts? Of course, that's the ideal, but it's not possible for everyone.

The need to maintain benefits is a prime reason many people remain chained to jobs they don't like. But you might be able to work around it. If you (and your family) are covered under your spouse or partner's health and benefits, then it won't be a big issue. To be fair, you might work out a deal with your partner in which you take turns working full-time (see chapter 9 for a real-life example of a couple who did just that).

Ideally, you'll be able to negotiate prorated benefits for your part-time position whether you're converting your full-time position to part-time or seeking a new part-time position (see chapter 5 on how to negotiate the best job and package).

If you're working without any benefits—whether as a consultant/freelancer, a small business owner, or a part-time employee—and you're not covered under any other plan (spouse/partner), you're going to have to view yourself as a contract worker. That means you will have to take care of yourself when it comes to things like insurance; and if you're an independent consultant, you're going to have to budget for the taxes you'll owe at the end of the year, as no one will automatically deduct them from your paycheck (see chapter 11 for more information on insurance and taxes).

Don't forget to save for the future. If you don't have retirement benefits, you're going to have to set up your own retirement fund—a variety of tax-favorable retirement accounts are available for individuals. If you're relying on your spouse's retirement package, you should look into what happens to those funds in the event of a divorce.

Also, don't forget to think about vacation and sick pay. Sometimes those are prorated for part-timers, but if they're not, you'll have to make sure your budget can handle a lack of cash flow during those times. (See chapter 4 for information on the rights of part-time employees in the United States, or more properly, the lack of any defined rights.)

If your first response to these tough issues is negative, don't pull back yet. There are pluses. If you adjust your life to a part-time schedule, you have more time in your life to enjoy yourself and to nurture your health and that of your family members. Working like a dog sixty hours a week with a measly two-week paid vacation a year often leaves people sick, tired, and spending money on things they don't want or need. That's why you really need to take a good hard look at what you're giving up and what you're gaining when you consider making the switch to becoming a part-time professional.

> ## Look at the Big Picture
>
> When looking at financial issues, you really need to weigh what you gain personally compared with what you think you might lose financially. For example, I know people who waited until retirement to start "enjoying life," only to discover that they were no longer healthy enough to live the life of their dreams. They worked themselves into chronic illness, or sometimes they worked themselves to death! (We've all heard stories of people dying shortly after retirement.) So, yes, you need to save for the future, but don't wait to start living your life. Go after what you want now, while you're reasonably healthy.

Does Part-Time Work Match Your Professional and Life Goals?

This is not an easy question, and it's one we deal with throughout the book, especially when I help you identify your values, skills, and interests. A simple place to start is to ask yourself the all-important questions: Why do you work? What role does work play in your life?

A. solely financial
B. mentally challenging
C. socially rewarding
D. spiritually rewarding
E. a physical outlet

If your answer is a combination of some or all of the above, then rank them in importance.

You'd be surprised how many people don't know or don't admit the answer to these questions. For example, I know someone who worked only for the money—and for a very specific amount. She only needed extra money for health insurance because her husband was an independent contractor without medical coverage. She knew exactly what her insurance bill was per month and that's the amount of money she sought to make in her part-time endeavors. If you're working solely for the money—you have the toughest road, but you also have the clearest goals.

If you're working part-time because you want to keep active in the world, want to keep your resume up to date, or simply need that outside pat on the back for self-esteem, then you have more options. The first thing you should look at when you consider a job is: does this match my interests? Does this match what I need in terms of stimulation and self-esteem?

To help determine your goals, take a closer look at the challenges of working part-time. For example, if you want to head your big-time prestigious law firm, then working part-time will most likely not get you there. If, however, you'd like to practice law—but let's say only twenty hours a week—and still have time left for family and life, that can be accomplished.

If you want to run for state senator, will reenvisioning your view of full-time and part-time work get you there? It could. Maybe you could cut back on your "real" job hours so you can follow your political passions in your spare time. You will still have time management issues because, in effect, you'll be working two part-time jobs. You will still have a question of life balance when it comes to family, self-care, relaxation, etc., but at least you will be moving down a path that more closely matches your life with your hopes, dreams, and ambitions.

You need to take a clear, hard look at how your professional mobility and growth will be affected if you take a part-time position. It may be that if you pick the right part-time position, your mobility and growth will increase tenfold. A recent study discussed in chapter 1 found that part-time workers did not pay a price in compensation and promotions. However, some perceive that their long-term career goals may be compromised if they work part-time. You'll need to examine your field carefully and do some research. Are you working in an old-school culture? Can you find any people in your field who have gone part-time? Are you looking at the current situation or relying on stories from ten years ago? Remember, the workplace environment is changing and corporations are adapting to handle shortages in quality workers.

Ask yourself the following questions:

- What are your short- and long-term goals, both professional and personal? This is not an easy question. Get out a notebook and keep it handy. Make your list over the course of several months—new ideas will crop up, and you'll scratch others off the list.
- How will making a move to part-time affect your professional growth? Will it hamper your promotability? If so, are you ready to suffer the consequences?
- How will working fewer hours open up your life in other ways professionally and personally? Remember, if you're going into a field that better suits your interests, this change may open many doors for growth, energy, and happiness.

What's Your Personality Type, and How Does It Fit with Part-Time Work?

The best part-time work draws on activities you enjoy, plays to your skills and talents, motivates you, and fits in with your preferred work style. Certain types of people are very well suited to working part-time. These people usually prefer flexibility, like a varied life, have many interests, are self-directed and self-disciplined, and like change. If you haven't had your personality type analyzed yet with a popular test such as the Myers-Briggs Type Indicator® personality inventory, contact your local adult education center or career counselor for more information. Abbreviated versions of the test are available on the Internet. Many are reasonably priced and can help you understand yourself and define your goals. The prices range from a one-time testing fee to consultation fees for working with a qualified counselor.

I recommend you consider meeting with a trained professional counselor to assess your results. Such a person can explain in detail what the results mean to and for you in the short and longer term. Solely reading results with no interpretation can be misleading and dangerous.

Most important, a Savvy Part-Time Professional is someone who is clear and focused and has a sense of direction in his or her work. To be successful working part-time, you must be determined and strong-willed regarding your needs and goals. You must have a clear mission and agenda in both areas. It is extremely helpful to be highly organized and have excellent time management skills. Being organized is a gift and talent that I believe can be developed (see chapter 11, Tools for Success).

Here are some personality-related issues to consider when deciding whether to go part-time:

- Other full-time employees where you work may resent you for your great lifestyle. Would you be affected by that, or do you have the confidence to follow your own path? You can compensate for office envy by demonstrating to your employer and co-workers that you still get your assigned job done in your allotted hours and by always honoring your responsibilities. However, some may resent you for getting more work done in four hours than they do in eight. Are you sensitive to that kind of office gossiping or sniping? If so, can you overcome your sensitivity?
- When you work part-time, you work fewer hours but often work harder than people who stretch out eight-hour days with endless coffee breaks and long chats around their neighbor's desk. Are you the type of person who can stay focused and get the job done, or do you require frequent breaks and distractions?
- If you work at home, how will you handle the distractions of kids, TV, telephone calls, and the Internet? No one is

looking over your shoulder—do you have the discipline to get your work done in a time-efficient manner? Can you draw a clear line between work time and play time? How will you set up your office? How will you define your rules? (See chapter 11, Tools for Success.)

- If you don't receive benefits through work, do you have the initiative and discipline to follow through on making sure you're covered for insurance, taxes, and retirement funds?
- Do you have the ability to switch gears easily from work to your personal responsibilities and vice versa, or do you need the cushion of transitional activities?

Can You Deal with Risk?

This is a key question to success in both life and work. We need to accept that all of us have what the Strong Interest Inventory Profile® refers to as a risk-taking score. Some of us dislike risk taking and prefer quiet activities and playing it safe, while others seek out adventure, appreciate original ideas, enjoy thrilling activities, and take chances. We need to be aware of this and accept it. Change is harder for some than others.

Even individuals who dislike taking risks and prefer to play it safe can learn how to make their lives richer and more fulfilling by beginning with small risks (baby steps) to change their current situation. You can achieve this by learning how to make better decisions and to take appropriate, not unreasonable, risks. Making a decision that may be seen as risky can be difficult for many reasons. In this book, you'll learn different ways to make the best decisions for yourself, and how others have made positive life-enhancing decisions.

The Changing Definition of Risk

Risk takes on different meanings as you move through the various stages of life. At some point, you may find that not taking a risk may actually be riskier than taking one. You may live to regret missed opportunities. If you don't search and you don't ask, you already know the answer.

When you were young, you may have thought of risk as merely physical—sky diving, rock climbing, driving fast cars. Now, however, taking a risk might mean taking a class in art, even though you think you're terrible at art, or applying for a job that you know you would enjoy but think it doesn't pay enough or have enough status. Or taking a risk might mean starting your own business or reducing your hours at work. It's important to reassess periodically your own personal definition of risk and challenge yourself to be more open to the idea of taking considered risks.

Obstacles and Mistakes

Just try to imagine yourself sitting someplace, several years from now, pondering your life and career. Which would make you feel better? Knowing that you tried, even if it involved some hardship and possibly even some mistakes? The more successful people are, it seems, the more mistakes they make. Errors often turn out to be more valuable down the road than the expected outcome. Did you know about the chemist who was trying to cook up a strong glue and thought he failed? His "mistaken" result is the adhesive used by millions daily on the back of "Post-it" notes.

As you go through your decision-making process, you will encounter obstacles and make mistakes. How you evaluate the obstacles and deal with the mistakes will determine the success of your endeavor.

We must develop faith and trust in the process and in what Susan Jeffers, in her book, *Feel the Fear and Do it Anyway*, calls the "higher self." If something doesn't work out as you imagined, look beyond it and understand the positives associated with it. For example, a client of mine applied to a doctoral program in psychology. She was not accepted, so, instead of at-

tending graduate school, she went into her own business. Today she has a viable business. It had appeared that she had
missed an opportunity, but she ended up creating something
profitable and fulfilling.

Mistakes can be your path to success by recognizing some
of the following:

- Acknowledge the fact that we all make mistakes.
- Don't worry about the details.
- Try to learn from your mistakes to grow.
- Share your mistakes with other people.
- Become focused. Mistakes frequently occur due to our
  current state of "multitasking".
- Don't be afraid of challenges, overcoming them is the only
  way to grow.

Try a "Try Out"

You don't need to jump into any endeavor with both feet and
no parachute. I always recommend to my clients that they have
a try-out experience, whether paid or unpaid, as a way to test
the waters. Before you jump into grad school for social work,
for instance, try volunteering to see if that sort of career is for
you. Or if you think you want to teach high school, try substitute teaching for at least a few days. The same philosophy holds
true for part-time work.

If you're starting from an unemployed position, this is the
perfect time to experiment with part-time. Can you get the job
you want? Can you afford it? Is it satisfying your life and career
needs? If you're working full-time, try to arrange for a sabbatical (see chapters 4 and 5) and take a stab at part-time work,
even if it's at a lower pay-scale. You'll have time to work on a
budget and life goals to see if you can afford it. Are the trade-
offs worth it? Is the time gained worth the potential income
lost? Have you really lost income if you've reduced your expenses?

Can You Deal with Change?

Change is good for you. How many times have you heard that and not felt it? Perhaps you don't like change, or you're scared of it or don't know how to handle it. If so, you're not alone. Many people don't like change, or, let's say, they're not used to it. Many of us get comfortable with the status quo in our lives. However, whether we like change or not, we're all confronted with it throughout our lifetime. We choose some changes, others are forced on us.

If you know change is coming, terminating your old routine and the structure it provides can be daunting. You may begin to feel out of sorts, befuddled, and alone. This is perfectly natural. Feeling out of control is uncomfortable, but it does have its benefits, for example, when discovery happens, when we can make a change that opens up whole new ways of life. That is, if we learn to be open to change, not paralyzed by it.

Unfortunately, the mantra for numerous individuals is "the devil you know is better than the devil you don't know." The key is to understand that change is inevitable, whether sought or forced on us, so it's helpful to begin learning coping techniques now.

There are many things you can do to conquer your fear of change. It's helpful to know people who model positive change in their lives. Start to watch people who have made positive changes. Read about people you admire. Seek out those who have made changes in their lives and talk to them. Ask them questions. You'll find that many of them harbored similar fears and reservations. Think about times when you were scared to make a change and yet it worked for you. Build up a folder of successful and satisfying experiences you've had as a result of changing something.

Change Before You Have To

At a seminar I attended, a speaker recommended changing before you have to. It was an interesting idea because you don't feel the pressure that you have to change. It's a more subtle experience, and you are not reacting to your situation, but responding to it.

Here are tips for changing before you have to:

- Change things in your life that begin to stifle you.
- Be willing to dream and step out of your comfort zone.
- Look at your life and assess where it feels lacking or empty.
- If you feel alone, join a group or association in a field of interest.
- If you're feeling physically out of shape, take a dance or exercise class or take up a new sport.
- If you lack intellectual stimulation, consider enrolling in a class or applying for a degree.
- Perhaps you always wanted to start your own business. Instead of merely dreaming about it, at least take a class in how to start your own business. It will get the ball rolling.
- Get clear on where the gaps in your life are and begin to take action. The options are limitless, but remember—take small steps!

Lynn's Change Equation

Many times we feel stuck and unable to take action. If you have a process or plan to follow, it becomes easier. Try breaking down an overwhelming task or desire into manageable pieces. With the support of others—a friend, spouse, partner, or trusted professional—you will acquire strength and conviction to go through the process of change. As you progress, strength builds on strength, and action leads to more action.

The equation looks like this:

- Step 1—Realization one needs to make a change.
- Step 2—Break down the challenges into manageable pieces.
- Step 3—Build up the courage to take risks.

Each action is either confirmed or denied by your feelings

throughout the process. Each action confirmed makes you stronger and more convinced to go on or not. You may decide to come to a halt because you realize this may not be the best decision for you at this time.

In the next chapter, we look at how to make a career transition and how to make decisions.

Strategies for Handling Change

Change is clearly a journey—a transformative experience where enlightenment slowly happens. Here are some strategies to help you cope with and evaluate changes big or small:

- Set aside a regular time and a place to be alone.
- Keep a journal about your thoughts and feelings as they relate to the change.
- Give yourself adequate time to make the change; don't expect things to "work out" overnight.
- Use humor—it works, trust me. Whenever I'm in the midst of a stressful situation, I try to find the humor or irony in it.
- Have a support system of people who believe in you who encourage you to focus on the dream and motivate you.
- Have a mentor to help you through or find a role model to inspire you.

CHAPTER 3

Three Steps to a Successful Career Transition

This chapter focuses on three basic steps that comprise my recommended tools for a smooth career transition. These concepts can be applied to any career transition, whether you're moving from full-time to full-time, full-time to part-time, or any combination of these.

In today's rapidly changing world, it's unrealistic to expect to remain in one career throughout your life. Occupational movement is inevitable because of changes in the marketplace, our lifestyles, values, and desires. As a result, most people have several different careers in their lifetime.

The question is: "How can you achieve the most successful career transition?" The best way to solve this is to imagine you're creating and putting together the pieces of an intriguing, challenging, and rewarding puzzle. You'll need to examine, shift, and view each piece from a variety of perspectives. Once you're able to fit the pieces of your puzzle together, you'll have created the complete image, which in effect, will become your career.

You must understand that fulfillment will come to you only when the pieces of your professional and personal life are combined and become whole. Your choice of work, therefore, needs to be in line with your interests, skills, needs (financial and emotional), personality style, and value system.

I'll discuss each piece of the puzzle in detail and ask you to do self-assessment exercises. This isn't easy. You may not have all the answers immediately. The self-examination process takes time and requires thought; however, from a long-term career and life-planning perspective, the rewards greatly outweigh the amount of time and effort involved.

Step 1: Get to Know Yourself

You first need to do a self-assessment. Self-assessment is the process that enables you to become increasingly aware of your *interests, values, motivated skills, temperament, needs, limitations, standards*, and *background influences*. Because your interests, values, skills, and needs change over time, you must begin to learn about yourself in the present and understand who you are today, not yesterday or five years ago. Let's start.

HOW DO YOU IDENTIFY YOUR INTERESTS?

During the course of a day, your interests direct your behavior. For example, which sections of the newspaper do you read first? What Web sites do you visit daily? If you think about your interests in this way, it helps you define where your primary enthusiasms lie.

In addition, many standardized, highly valuable, and reliable testing instruments (e.g., the Strong Interest Inventory Profile®) enable you to measure these various components with greater sophistication. I highly recommend the Strong Interest Inventory Profile®; however, keep in mind that it needs to be administered by a trained certified counselor. An alternative way to understand yourself is to stop and ask what it is that you enjoy and what makes you happy. In general, people who share mutual passion for their occupations tend to be more satisfied and more productive.

Many people incorrectly assume that interests are something they can enjoy after work, and that these passions cannot be turned into paid work. For example, are you computer savvy? You could become a consultant and work at home. If you enjoy sports, you could work in sports marketing.

FURTHER RESOURCES

To find a certified career counselor or coach, consult the following sites:

- International Coach Directory, www.findacoach.com
- International Coach Federation, www.coachfeaderation.org
- National Board for Certified Counselors, www.nbcc.org

REAL-LIFE EXAMPLE

Kim is a perfect example of someone who figured out how to combine a career with her interests. Kim loves furniture, travel, and technology, but she never thought it would be possible to combine all three into a career. She started small by listing her furniture on eBay and hopes to open an antique furniture store one day, which would allow her to travel and shop for merchandise. Since she began this business, she continues to work in a more secure job until she feels comfortable enough to take the leap and invest herself completely in her new venture.

HOW DO YOU IDENTIFY YOUR VALUES?

Values are difficult to define and may change over time. Your values are those qualities of life that you find most attractive, important, and worthy of your attention. When engaged in activities that you value, you feel most like yourself. You feel connected, excited, and fulfilled. The first step is to be truthful with yourself about what you actually value in life. What do you value? Some examples include:

Power	Creating
Helping others	Discovering
Feeling good	Mastering activities
Moving forward	Pleasure
Connecting with people	Spirituality
Adventure	Feeling safe
Beauty	Winning
Leading people	Making social contributions

Sometimes it is easier to ask what you love to do with your time. If you're a parent, is it the ability to stay home with your children and watch them throughout their daily routines? Is it more important to take extended business trips to help promote your career? Is it the security of a steady stream of income? Is it the power of your old position? The professional status you have achieved? The freedom to leave home every day? There are no right or wrong answers to these questions; however, it is important to know that your answer will change as your life changes.

Ideally, you want the time and effort you spend on activities to be in line with your values, and you want your values to guide your decisions. To do this, you need to recognize your changing priorities. Life circumstances change, and how you allocate your time should change accordingly. You need to be honest with yourself as you continually fine-tune your priorities. If the importance of different roles shifts (you were a parent and now you're an empty nester), rebalance and reevaluate your time investments. Begin this process by identifying what is presently most significant to you, and then budget your time and choices accordingly.

It's often easier to look at your values in terms of money. Where would you want to spend your money? Prioritize the following according to their importance to you:

- success in your career
- friendships with others
- high-status job
- entrepreneurship
- self-confidence
- peace of mind
- healthy lifestyle
- volunteer/philanthropic activities
- financial security
- autonomy
- creativity

- adventure
- family time

HOW DO YOU IDENTIFY YOUR MOTIVATED SKILLS?

Think of a few accomplishments in your life that have given you satisfaction—they may be vocationally or avocationally related. For example, you may have done one of the following: organized a fund-raising activity for your favorite charity, created a beautiful piece of art, worked on an unusual project at work. There is usually a common thread that connects your professional and personal sense of achievement or satisfaction. This link is a motivator and provides you with the desire needed to succeed. These motivators help you quickly learn skills that are usually displayed in such different capacities as leadership, interpersonal relations, artistic ability, or mechanical or organizational endeavors and are generally transferable among different fields. Motivated skills make you feel proficient and give you enjoyment.

For example, look at each of the skills listed below and rate yourself accordingly: a) highly competent, b) competent, or c) have little proficiency. Then, rate how you find using these skills: a) enjoyable, b) tolerable, or c) unpleasant.

Which ones received the highest rating (highly competent and enjoyable), and which ones received the lowest rating (have little proficiency and unpleasant)? This simple exercise may help you understand the concept of using skills that are enjoyable and in which you are proficient—these are your motivated skills. For example, did you include any of these skills?

- speaking before groups
- producing events
- conceptualizing
- problem solving
- writing
- advocating
- organizing

- designing
- explaining
- working outdoors
- building
- analyzing
- training
- promoting
- selling
- computing
- delegating
- creating

A REAL-LIFE EXAMPLE

The experience of one of my clients highlights the value and distinction between using your motivated skills and relying solely on "just what you are good at." Suzy was a financial analyst at a major investment banking firm in New York City. She was extremely analytic and quite good at her job; however, she did not enjoy analyzing numbers all day—people inspired her more. After she conducted the above exercise, she decided to change careers. She made the transition into a counseling role and worked with people to help them discover what would add passion and satisfaction to their lives. She decided to go back to school and become a career counselor. Now, Suzy is combining her interpersonal and analytic skills, so she is excited and motivated to go to her job each day.

HOW DO YOU IDENTIFY YOUR PERSONALITY, STYLE, AND TEMPERAMENT?

As mentioned in chapter 2, when you work part-time it is helpful to be focused, somewhat open to risk and change, and flexible. To take it a step further it is beneficial to become comfortable and familiar with your temperament and personality preferences, which will make the transition easier.

A commonly used professional assessment instrument in the career-coaching field is the Myers-Briggs Type Indicator® (MBTI) personality inventory. This inventory measures your personality style and preferences to help you understand who you are. In the assessment, you are asked a series of questions that together paint a portrait of your personality traits. The MBTI aids in comprehending how you generally look at the world and attempts to define what types of decisions you tend to make relating to your personality. For example, The Myers-Briggs Type Indicator® personality inventory answers four major questions:

- Where do you prefer to focus your attention?
- How do you prefer to take in information?
- How do you make decisions?
- How do you deal with the outer world?

Knowing your preferences and learning about other people's preferences can help you become aware of your special strengths, work values, successes, and personal styles. The MBTI can also help you understand how people with different preferences can relate to each other and be valuable to society. As I said earlier, I highly recommend that you have the test administered by a trained professional counselor in private practice or affiliated with a credentialed organization.

You should also consider your work temperament. For instance, are you calm, excitable, sensitive, anxious, energetic? These qualities need to be taken into consideration when you think about your career choices.

REAL-LIFE EXAMPLE

Paul is a very energetic, positive person with an entrepreneurial spirit. He started working in a very conventional job at a highly conservative insurance company. His work was not in line with his temperament and was mismatched to his environment; it deenergized him and sapped his creativity. When he started looking for a new position, Paul understood the need to match his personality with his work atmosphere and is now employed by a financial firm in a job that draws more on his entrepreneurial nature. He is working as a salesman, which allows him to be more creative and resourceful in using his ideas and contacts. He no longer feels tired and drained, rather he feels stimulated and invigorated. Now, when he goes home to his family, he is calmer and can enjoy his time away from the office.

HOW DO YOU IDENTIFY YOUR NEEDS?

Your personal needs can include feeling accepted, accomplished, acknowledged, loved, cared for, in control, wanted, responsible, free, honest, ordered, peaceful, powerful, recognized, safe, etc. Needs are basic in that they have to be met for you to begin to move on to the next level, expressing your values.

REAL-LIFE EXAMPLE

For many years, Tom worked as an accountant in a privately owned firm. He felt very unsettled and insecure about his future within the company. Many of our conversations highlighted his need for security. As a result of his deeper understanding of and appreciation for feeling financially secure, he is exploring the possibility of getting a job in the federal government. As he explores his options, he is beginning to discover that a more secure job is better suited to his needs and personality style.

HOW DO YOU IDENTIFY YOUR STANDARDS?

These are your absolute requirements for happiness and fulfillment today. We need to adjust constantly to determine what we find acceptable and unacceptable. Your requirements are constantly evolving, and your professional and career goals should reflect these changes. Standards are very personal. For example, if you are highly concerned about the environment you need to work for a company whose environmental standards match your own. If you have high standards regarding academic achievement, you need to identify institutions and organizations that employ and appreciate employees with high levels of education.

HOW DO YOU IDENTIFY YOUR BACKGROUND INFLUENCES?

Our background influences are very powerful and can affect us positively or negatively for most of our lives. You should ask yourself, "Are my decisions based on my past influences or current desires?" For example, am I pursuing a career in medicine because several members of my family are doctors? Background influences can be motivators, but many people find them to be limiting as well.

However, when we act on a *desire*, we experience less friction and feel more honest and at peace with others and ourselves. It takes time to begin to trust what you want. For example, ask yourself simple questions such as, "Am I spending time with people out of obligation or desire?" "In my free time, do I do things I truly want to do?" Try asking yourself these questions throughout the day and analyze your answers; you may be surprised by how you spend most of your time. Do this exercise often, and you will begin identifying what you need to change or what you need to explore.

TRY OUT

After you put all these pieces together and come to a tentative objective, you might want to see if your puzzle is accurate. I recommend trying out your new attitude and ideas through a volunteer experience, internship, or simply taking classes at a local university. For example, if you are interested in children, volunteer at a local school as a mentor or tutor. If you love art, volunteer in a museum.

There are hundreds of ways you can try out different situations and settings. Be creative. Read all you can about the field. Subscribe to several magazines and related periodicals. Become involved with professional associations that will help educate you about your prospective field.

REAL-LIFE EXAMPLE

A client of mine currently works in an office setting, but he is considering making the transition to construction and working outdoors. He decided to spend time on the weekends assisting a local contractor. As an added bonus, the contractor is repaying his gratitude by helping my client out with some repairs on his own house.

REAL-LIFE EXAMPLE: MY STORY

I'd like to share some information about myself. I've made several occupational choices during my lifetime, and the most important and influential choices have been those that I took the time and effort to explore thoroughly. I'm the first person to say this is not an easy task, and you will not find your answers immediately. The self-assessment process is time-consuming and requires deep thought and proper motivation. But if you take the time to get to know yourself, ideas and solutions will become apparent in your life. Think of this process as a treasure hunt. You need to dive deep and unravel layer after layer to get to the hidden treasure. The process can be lengthy, but the rewards are great.

Step 2: Make Room for Growth

The second step involves making room in your life for this new beginning. It's important to create space and clear pathways as you prepare to change and grow. Organizing your life will energize you. Identify and eliminate those unnecessary papers on your desk, remove clothes from your closet that you have been saving and will never wear again. When you get rid of all the things that fill up space in your life, you'll be able to welcome new opportunities and experiences that will revitalize you.

Some questions to ask yourself:

- Are your personal files, papers, and receipts saved on your computer or filed away?
- Is your home neat and clean? Do you live in an environment you love and that makes you feel good?

- Do you surround yourself with things that are beautiful to you, that you like to see, smell, or touch?
- Is there anything in your home you want to change or remove?
- Is your work setting productive and inspiring?
- Do you have adequate time, space, and freedom right now?

Think about your overall well-being in terms of daily habits or rituals that nurture your health and your spirit. Strength and vitality can be seen physically and emotionally. A person who takes care of himself or herself is more productive and is viewed as valuable to his or her employer.

Some questions to ask are:

- Do you have adequate exercise and physical activity in your life?
- Is there something you do that you look forward to every day?
- Do you rush or use any adrenaline throughout your day?
- Are you taking care of any emotional problems you may have?

Are your financial affairs in order? This does not mean that you should be independently wealthy, have the perfect retirement nest egg, paid off you mortgage, etc. What it does mean is that you should know where you stand financially. Ask yourself:

- What is my net worth?
- Do I know what I spend my money on? Can I limit expenditures in any way?
- Do I need to consolidate and pay off debt?
- How much money do I need to meet my needs and the needs of my family?
- How much money do I want to meet my desires and the desires of my family?

- Are my financial papers organized?
- Do I understand my insurance coverage, tax situation, savings plans?
- Do I need to consult a professional financial adviser?

Last, surround yourself with supportive people and let them in on your newfound self and your plan for change. Read enriching motivational books and speak with people who have made similar changes in their lives. Let go of relationships that drag you down or damage or immobilize you. Work on developing a supportive network of people who appreciate you for who you are and challenge you to become who you want to be.

Step 3: Keep Your Eyes on the Prize

The third step in achieving a smooth career transition involves maintaining your focus, perseverance, and motivation. Remember, this process takes time; fulfillment and awareness don't happen overnight.

It's useful to approach this process slowly and take each day as it comes. Keep the project in perspective and allow it to build upon itself. I recommend that my clients fulfill daily goals. It is helpful to establish a plan with simple action steps that will lead you through each step of the process. This journey should be exciting and informative and shouldn't be an additional pressure in your life, so take it slow.

VISUALIZE

Here's an exercise to help you envision the future you want: Think ahead five or ten years and visualize your life as if it had already happened. Can you see yourself? You are in your ideal job. What are you doing? How do you feel? What do your physical surroundings look like? Are they busy or relaxed? Are you alone or with other people? If there are people around, what kind of people are they? What types of activities are you involved in? Are you the boss, or do you have a boss? Do you supervise anyone? How are you dressed? Are you comfortable? Are you in a small or a large company; is it your own company? How do you get to work, and how long does it take you? What time are you home at night? How do you spend your lunch hour and with whom? What are your hours? Answering some of these questions can be helpful in determining what it is you want to do. Visualization can be a highly effective technique for helping to create a picture of what you want.

Think about the above exercise—what were your reactions? Did you find out some information you didn't know about yourself? How specific was your visualization? What did it feel like to create that picture in your head? As mentioned, visualization can be a highly effective technique in gaining clarity and focus toward your goals. Once you have begun to see your future, it is easier to work toward reaching it.

HOW TO MAKE DECISIONS

Any transition or change involves decision making, and people make decisions in many different ways—from totally superficial to deeply considered. It may be fun to put on a different hat and experiment with a method that's not your usual style. Remember, we learn as much from our failures (maybe more) as we do from our successes.

That said, however, the best decisions are value-based. As a Savvy Part-Time Professional, you are trying to design and live your life in such a way that you are living your values. The part-time position you choose, you hope, is one that will allow you to honor and express your values.

EIGHT WAYS TO MAKE A DECISION

Now that you have more clarity about yourself and need to make a decision, here are eight ways people make decisions. This list should give you some alternatives to experiment with as you begin the decision-making process. Whatever you choose or whatever combination you explore, keep in mind your values as discussed in this chapter. What do you really need from life:

money, satisfaction, flexibility, excitement? Never lose sight of your values.

1. Gather as much information about yourself as you can, then do what I call "people and book research." People research includes speaking to as many people as possible who have made decisions similar to yours. Book research includes researching written and Internet materials related to your decision.
2. Visualize the possibilities and the projected outcomes. For example, try to visualize your life now, in three months, nine months, and one year. Which options will serve you best now and in the future?
3. Make a list of advantages and disadvantages of each potential outcome. The tricky part of this approach is that you are making a conscious choice about priorities, and you need to think about what is most important to you.
4. Build a team of supportive people, carefully selected for their expertise, and ask them for their advice.
5. Spend quiet time alone reflecting on the subject.
6. Evaluate feelings at every point of the decision-making process as you progress along your path.
7. Professional life coach Diana Robinson suggests tossing a coin. "As you observe how it falls, check out your feelings. Do you feel happier or wish you hadn't made the toss? The answer will tell you which way you really want to go, and you are not bound by the fall of the coin."
8. If all else fails, try the old rock, paper, scissors game—the children's game similar to one-two-three shoot. In this game, the hand signal for a rock breaks (and therefore wins over) scissors, scissors cuts paper, and paper hides the rock. Don't laugh; journalist Carol Vogel reported in the *New York Times* that "In Japan, resorting to such games of chance is not unusual." The president of an electronics company based outside of Japan recently used this method when he couldn't decide whether Christie's or Sotheby's should sell an art collection worth more than $20 million.

HOW TO FEEL PERSONALLY EMPOWERED

When you meet someone who is truly confident, that confidence is obvious right away. Most likely, that person has taken charge of his or her life and is reaping the benefits. That doesn't mean that person has achieved all of his or her goals. But that person is on the right path, doing what he or she wants. When you take risks and/or make difficult decisions, you start to become personally empowered and start experiencing the benefits of that empowerment in your life. It is also easier to make decisions when you feel personally empowered.

Here are ways to feel empowered:

- Start taking actions, but do so with baby steps. That's how most of us learned to walk and how some us have become marathon runners. Remember, strength builds strength and action leads to action.
- Live in the present. Begin to make the most of your life and try to live it to the fullest.
- Give yourself space to be quiet and calm.
- Observe what is holding you back. Many times we fight what doesn't come naturally to us. The next time you find yourself contesting something, ask yourself what's in it for you to explore more. This is what I call our "blocks and obstacles," things that hold us back. We need to ask ourselves whether they are real or imagined.
- Don't give in mindlessly to overly emotional reactions. Learn some conflict management skills and try to go with the flow. In other words, conserve your energy for what really matters.
- Keep your eyes on the prize. Stay focused on your goals and needs. Don't let things that happened in the past drag you down. Move forward. You can't change or control the past, but you can exert reasonable influence on the present and the future.
- Be as kind as possible to yourself.
- Look at life from a long-term horizon and recognize changing priorities.

- Reevaulate decisions and plans. After you view all the options and have taken some actions, you might end up not going ahead with your plan.

YOUR GOAL SHEET

Now that you've taken a hard look at your values and interests, it's time to take some action to make the changes in your life happen. A fellow coach shared this goal sheet with me many years ago, and I think it's a simple but effective tool. Write down three personal and three professional goals you'd like to accomplish in the next three months. Then list two action steps for each goal that will move you in the right direction. Don't be afraid to take "baby" action steps. In fact, it's smarter to start with small, achievable goals than to write down the impossible.

For example, if a personal goal is to make more friends, the first step (action step 1) might be to put together a list of clubs or activities that interest you. The second step (action step 2) could be attending a meeting or event related to one of those groups.

A business goal might be to cut down on time spent at the office. Your first step might be to read and do the exercises in this book. Your second step might be to start a file on part-time opportunities.

1. Personal Goal:
   - Action Step 1:

   - Action Step 2:

2. Personal Goal:
   - Action Step 1:

   - Action Step 2:

3. Personal Goal:
   - Action Step 1:

   - Action Step 2:

—— —— —— —— —— —— —— —— —— ——

1. Business Goal:
   - Action Step 1:

   - Action Step 2:

2. Business Goal:
   - Action Step 1:

   - Action Step 2:

3. Business Goal:
   - Action Step 1:

   - Action Step 2:

CHAPTER 4

Options for Part-Time Work

There's no single definition of part-time work. It could mean working one hour a week or thirty hours a week. It could mean working a flexible schedule, working part of the year, working as an independent contractor, or job sharing. According to attorney Judith Moldover, there is actually "no definition, legal or otherwise, of part-time work that applies to all employees in all workplaces" (see Employment Rights of Part-Time Employees at the end of this chapter). In this chapter I review the terminology applied to a variety of part-time positions, as well as the advantages and challenges of each, so you can determine which option might work best for you. I also provide some tips for dealing with each particular option. All part-time positions have the advantage of more personal time, better work/life balance, and greater flexibility, so I don't repeat those under each section. Nor do I list as a challenge lower pay and fewer benefits than a full-time position, as that generally goes without saying, unless you find or create a position that pays more than your previous full-time job. With the money issue, you also have to remember, as we discussed in chapter 1, that you have significant savings in day care and commuting, depending on your situation and schedule.

Permanent Part-Time Employee

A permanent part-time employee is a person who works as an *employee* of a company or individual, but who works less than a defined full-time schedule. Prorated benefits may or may not be included. Job sharing is also considered a form of permanent part-time work (see the next section).

The schedule for part-time workers can also vary with the needs of the company. For example, if you work for a tax company, you may end up working full-time from January through April, then return to reduced hours the rest of the year.

Being employed by a company as a designated part-time employee can be a good choice for those who like the utmost stability and predictability in their life. This may also be the best choice for those who need steady paychecks and health and retirement benefits. Government positions, large corporations, or well-established companies are often the best sources for these kinds of jobs. What they lack in salary potential and excitement, they make up for in a certain amount of security. Even the "big," slow-moving bureaucracies are taking advantage of new attitudes toward flextime; however, even with that, highly structured companies tend to be the least flexible when it comes to working with employees individually. They often have too many employees and too many structures in place to tailor schedules to specific needs.

Conversely, smaller companies tend to lag in the benefits department, but they try to make up for this by offering more flexibility, growth potential, and, possibly, a more casual atmosphere.

My suggestion: If you're working solely for the money and benefits, make sure you're getting the best deal possible. If you're not having fun, fulfilling a creative urge, building toward specific career goals, getting optimal flexibility, or otherwise satisfying some other lifestyle need, such as ease of commute or having the benefit of a casual low-stress position, then you might as well be making the most you can. If your company or employer doesn't offer benefits to part-time employees, consider finding one that does.

Advantages of working as a permanent part-time employee for a specific company or individual:

- Similar to a full-time employee in that part-timers get a steady paycheck, work dependable hours, and have a company to take care of expenses, office supplies, office support for computers, and withholding taxes.
- Better chance of securing prorated benefits, including health and retirement benefits, and sick and vacation days.
- Gives you a chance to get out of the house and work with other people. Get to be part of the social aspects of work— holiday parties, conferences; gives you a feeling of having a "place" in the world.
- More opportunities to take part in company-funded training.

Challenges of working as a permanent part-time employee for a specific company or individual:

- Possibility of fewer responsibilities or fewer opportunities for promotion (this one is also debatable as workplace culture and goals change; see highlights from a 2005 study on the subject in chapter 1).
- Possible resentment from full-time co-workers.
- Hours and pay reduced but duties may stay the same (employer tries to cram a full-time job into a part-time position).
- May have to work harder and more intensely during your limited hours, which may lead to burnout.
- May be the first to go in "lean" times.
- If you work for a large company or government entity, you may have limited flexibility in designing your schedule.

Tips on working as a permanent part-time employee for a specific company or individual:

- Set clear terms with your employer regarding responsibilities/pay/benefits/promotions.
- Continually sell the advantages to the company of working part-time.
- Know your limits. Don't take on more work than you can

do in your new part-time hours. You will need to learn to say no tactfully.

- Take advantage of technology—emails, Blackberry, cell phones, video phones, conference calling—all of these have made it much easier to keep up with people without requiring face-to-face encounters.

- Have a plan when meetings or other important events are scheduled on your day off; try to be flexible and responsive to your company.

- Be prompt, efficient, and accessible when dealing with everyone, including fellow staffers. (If there's a crisis, make sure they know how to reach you on your days out of the office.)

- Draw boundaries for yourself, but be adaptable and flexible. If someone really needs your input and it's your day off, give the person an answer if you can. If you feel like someone is taking advantage of you or pulling this trick once too often, then take a stand. But sometimes people really do need a prompt response.

- Don't gloat over your newfound freedom with the full-timers. Keep a low profile and don't brag how great life is now that you can enjoy a bigger part of the day.

- Stay current in your field; network with the appropriate people and organizations; lobby hard to take part in any training opportunities, conferences, etc.

- If you're not getting what you want from your employer, start investigating other opportunities.

REAL-LIFE EXAMPLE: PART-TIME SENIOR EDITOR

Susan, a senior editor, was working as a freelancer for a company two to three days a week when they asked her if she could work full-time. She was very interested in the position; however, for personal reasons she could only work four days per week. At that point, she asked if this was a possibility and the company agreed. This has been her situation for the past twenty-seven years. The art director and her other colleagues know

> ## A Wolf in Sheep's Clothing
>
> Beware of supposed part-time positions that are really full-time jobs in sheep's clothing, that is, thirty or thirty-five plus hours a week with no benefits. These are money-strapped or cheap employers that are trying to get a full-time worker without having to fork over the money or benefits. The pressure and frustration could negate the benefits of having an extra five or ten hours of free time. This is why you need to learn how to become a Savvy Part-Time Professional—in other words, how to become your own best advocate! The secret: know yourself and what you want and need out of life and your professional career.

she doesn't work on Fridays and make the appropriate adjustments. In a pinch, she brings work home, but this rarely occurs, because she usually accomplishes her work in the allotted time.

Her week is set up so she has a full weekend to relax because she has the opportunity to do her errands and chores on Friday, which is a major benefit of a four-day workweek. This also gives her the opportunity to visit the gym more often and stay physically active and in good shape.

She feels lucky to have found a situation that works for her. Not receiving a paycheck for the fifth day of work is a trade-off, but she believes it's been worth it. Her success is due to her discipline, talent, and organizational abilities.

The key point to remember is that she asked for the four-day-a-week schedule and she got it. It never hurts to ask—you may be pleasantly surprised.

REAL-LIFE EXAMPLE: PART-TIME SENIOR EXECUTIVE

In 1982, after raising her children, Sandra went back to work for a large nonprofit organization. She was referred by an individual who knew her through her volunteer activities. Originally, she worked two days a week, but then her work schedule was increased to four days a week. She told the organization that she would never work five days a week, and they agreed to this arrangement.

The fifth day of each week she spends as a volunteer, her labor of love. Her passions, which include Jewish issues, women's rights, leadership, and the changing world, are all satisfied.

The biggest advantage of working part-time is that it allows her the time to satisfy all parts of herself and it gives her the bonus of a three-day weekend. However, it can prove to be a challenge not being in her office full-time. There are times when she has to bring work home, but thanks to technology she can accomplish quite a bit on her computer.

Job Sharing

Job sharing is when two employees split a full-time position. The two employees have an agreed-upon schedule and division of responsibilities. This situation is often a very good bet for demanding professional positions, which can't easily be pared down into a part-time schedule.

If you can figure out a way to divide up the job into specific responsibilities, your job may be sharable. The first step is to answer these questions:

- Is it possible to divide specific job responsibilities?
- How many of the tasks are time sensitive? How many aren't?
- Will internal staff or external clients be able to deal with the situation?

Your next step is to determine the schedule. The possibilities are almost limitless. Some split the schedule fifty-fifty, but other arrangements can be worked out as well. Here are some scheduling options:

- Alternating three days/two days per week
- Splitting each day 50/50

- Each person works three days with one day overlapping (this option ensures good communication and efficient work flow and transfer of responsibilities)
- One week on, one week off

All variations can be worked out. To be most successful, however, you want to communicate regularly with customers, clients, managers, and staff so everyone knows who is working and when. You always need to think about all contingencies. If one has a family emergency or is sick, is the other on call? If one job sharer resigns, what are the consequences? Under what situation is one partner responsible if the other is unable to fulfill his or her responsibilities? You also need to think about your personality style and how it best fits in a job share situation.

- Do you like to share in decision making, responsibilities, and results?
- Can you negotiate and compromise well?

Advantages of job sharing:

- Best bet for securing a highly professional part-time job, that is, doctor, accountant, etc.
- Good bet for getting prorated benefits.
- Two sets of experience and skill for one job.
- The position is always covered, including during vacations and sick days.
- Clients and staff have consistent access to the responsible person.
- Having someone to share ideas with can create a real synergy of talent and energy.
- In an emergency situation, you have a replacement.

Challenges include:

- Finding a job share partner with whom you work well. Make

sure you're familiar with the person—his or her work style, personality. If you don't know the candidate personally, get references and check them. Spend some time with the candidate via lunches, dinners, etc.

- Finding the right company and position. Moving from an established position to a job share is the best bet. Give your job share proposal a lot of thought before you propose it to management (see chapter 5).
- Having to share credit.
- Going through the process of restructuring the job.
- The responsibility of making schedules and tasks work is in the hands of the job sharing-team, so you need to be organized and motivated and not blame your problems on other staff or management.
- If one person quits, you may suddenly find yourself either out of a job or back in a full-time job, so you need to plan for all contingencies.

Tips on successful job sharing:

- Communicate with your partner routinely. This is probably the most important factor for success. Don't rely solely on phone calls and emails. If you don't overlap in the office, meet at least once a month for lunch or coffee.
- Communicate regularly with all staff members and clients.
- Keep a shared calendar of events, meetings, deadlines, etc.
- Keep a written list of projects and "things to do."
- Don't forget to change your voice mail to reflect your job-sharing status.
- Arrange your office and all files—hard and electronic—so each of you knows exactly where everything is.
- Maintain a shared list of contacts, phone numbers, etc.
- Decide in advance who will attend which meetings. Will you alternate? Remember, getting your share of "face" time with important staff and clients is crucial.

- Determine how work will be evaluated. What happens if one person is doing more work or is performing better than the other?
- Network with other job sharers; keep up-to-date on advice, ideas, problem solving.

RESOURCES

- http://workoptions.com/jobshare.htm
- http://www.opm.gov/Employment_and_Benefits/WorkLife/ OfficialDocuments/handbooksguides/PT_Employ_ JobSharing/pt08.asp

REAL-LIFE EXAMPLE: JOB SHARE

Joyce, a career counselor, worked at a psychological rehabilitation center in a job share. She decided to work part-time because she had young children at home. Her schedule included working twenty hours, or two and a half days, a week. She and her job share partner worked one overlapping day so they could share information. The reward of her job share situation was that she had more personal time.

During her entire time in the position, she never felt totally integrated in her role and visible in the organization. The experience was isolating for her. When her job share partner resigned, she decided to resign as well because she felt she had lost her anchor. In retrospect, if Joyce had felt more comfortable and confident, she would have created another job share situation because the concept was great and the situation worked well for her at that stage of her career.

The tips she offered were to establish good communication with your partner and take advantage of the overlap day to share information.

Flextime and the Compressed Workweek

Flextime can apply to both full- and part-time positions. If you can't work less, working under a flexible schedule is the next best thing. Flextime allows employees to choose, within set limits, the times they start and finish work. Everyone works best at different times of the day. Some people are more productive in the early hours, others late in the day. Under a flextime arrangement you can choose and alter your schedule to suit your preferred work style; it also allows you to take care of personal responsibilities when you need to. This can foster high productivity and efficiency.

The *compressed work week* is full-time work but can give you an extra day to run errands, go to the doctor, volunteer at your child's school, or simply relax. In this model, a forty-hour workweek is compressed into less than five days—usually four ten-hour days with one day off, generally a Friday, or five nine-hour days in one week followed by four nine-hour days the next with every other Friday off. The advantage is obvious in that you get the extra day off. But some find it difficult to work longer days.

Advantages of the compressed workweek:

- More personal time
- Extra day off

Challenges of the compressed workweek:

- Very long days can lead to burnout

Tips for the compressed workweek:

- Don't try to compress schedule too much; know your limits.
- Start slowly, then build up to longer days.

Another twist on flextime is something called "core hours." In this situation, you agree to be at the office for a key period of time, say ten o'clock to four o'clock, but other than that, you can come in when you want and leave when you want, as long as your eight hours are covered.

Telecommuting or Telework

With telecommuting, sometimes called telework, the employee works from home on a predetermined basis. Sometimes an employee works almost exclusively from home, at other times as little as once a week. Schedules are often determined on a case-by-case basis. This setup can work well for both part- and full-time employees. Most people get this type of arrangement after they've been working at a company or within a particular field for a certain length of time. They have proven themselves, so employers trust them to get the job done from home.

However, advances in technology and growing flexibility and creativity in the workplace are opening up more opportunities for telecommuting, especially as roads in metropolitan areas become increasingly snarled by traffic and gas prices increase. The savings in commuting costs can be significant for employees. In fact, according to a 2005 *Washington Post* article, the surge in gas prices after hurricanes Katrina and Rita led to a significant rise in the number of telecommuters. Basically, if your job involves a lot of time on the phone or computer, you're a good candidate for telecommuting (see How to Negotiate a Telecommuting Contract in chapter 5).

Advantages of telecommuting include:

- Dependable paycheck (unlike independent consultant work) and the possibility of prorated benefits.
- Save significant money: lower travel expenses and fewer hours lost to commuting; less work-appropriate clothing, fewer purchases and lower dry cleaning expenses; lunch at home saves time and money; savings on child care expenses, etc.
- Increased flexibility in dealing with your chores and enjoying your pleasures.
- Greater ease in dealing with family member appointments/ illnesses.

Challenges of telecommuting include:

- Need space in your home to work.
- If children are home, need to find a quiet place. Children need to learn not to interrupt except for an emergency.
- Lack of office time and face time with key players can leave you out of the loop and thus out of consideration for promotions, training, raises.
- Loneliness.
- Higher utility costs.
- Supervisors may doubt your trustworthiness until you've proven yourself.

Tips for telecommuting include:

- Your home office must be conducive to working efficiently and have proper equipment, including a good telephone setup (adequate phone lines), a computer, fax, and high-speed Internet connection. Be clear on who will pay for your computer expenses, phone bill, etc. Have a plan in place for when the inevitable equipment problems pop up. Does the company want you to use its repair service? How will you be reimbursed?
- Visit the office at least once a month. Determine with your employers in advance how often they want to meet face-to-face.
- You need to be keenly aware that you must update your co-workers and supervisors about your work assignments and progress.
- Determine how your projects will be assigned and how you will be supervised and evaluated.
- Get everything you can in writing.
- Be aware of Instant Messaging programs or other systems that show that you're "idle" at your computer.
- Carry your cell phone or a cordless phone around the house with you, so your employer can always get in touch with you during assigned working hours.

- Did I say communicate? Communicate. Communicate. Communicate.

RESOURCES

There are many telecommuting job sites out there, most of which charge a fee to search for jobs. Just enter "telecommuting" in an Internet search and many will come up. The following associations offer resources and tips:

- The American Telecommuting Association, http://www.knowledgetree.com/ata.html
- A long list of telecommuting resources available from the Working Moms Refuge Web site, www.momsrefuge.com/telecommute/resources/index.html
- Telework Coalition, www.telcoa.org
- Washington Metropolitan Area Telework Centers, www.wmtc.org. Although this is a regional site, it has good information on the benefits of telework, including a "savings calculator" to help you figure out how much gas money you'll save and by how much you'll reduce pollution.

Independent Contractor or Freelance Worker

Another option includes working as an independent contractor or freelancer. Attorney Judith Moldover provides the following description of a part-time consultant:

> If you are a part-time consultant, you are not an employee at all. Most legal rights you have will come from your agreement with your client. You should have a written agreement because oral agreements are not enforceable in court in most states if they cannot be performed in one year. A signed letter or series of letters can create an enforceable contract, but it is usually better to have a formal agreement. Consultants may legally be eligible to participate in a client's executive compensation plans,

but the client's plan design determines the extent of participation, if any. To be a true consultant (i.e., an independent contractor), you must run your own business with no client input into how you accomplish your results. There are various tests to determine independent contractor status under federal law. If your client classifies you as a consultant, but in reality you are a part-time employee, your "client" is subject to penalties by federal, state, and local taxing authorities for failing to withhold employment taxes. You may also be eligible for any employee benefits and wages which you should have received as a part-time employee.

Advantages of working as an independent contractor or freelance worker include:

- You can arrange your own schedule.
- You are the boss.
- Freedom—you're not stuck in an office all day.
- In good economic times you can choose your clients/work.

Challenges of working as an independent contractor or freelance worker include:

- It can be hard to find consistent work.
- It can be difficult in bad economic times.
- You always need to market your skills.
- Lack of benefits—you need to self-insure and save for retirement.
- You need to withhold your own taxes, which means you'll probably need to file quarterly estimates or prepay some taxes (check with a qualified professional).
- You need to budget for the ups and downs of the business cycle.

Tips for working as an independent contractor or freelance worker include:

- To be an independent contractor, you need to organize your life. Time management is crucial.
- Have a solid business plan with backup contingencies.
- Know yourself and your work style. Are you self-disciplined, self-motivated, innovative, resilient, and resourceful? You'll need all those skills.
- It's also very important to stay abreast of work in your field.
- Develop a deep list of clients or potential clients.
- Network, network, network!!
- Know comparable salaries and rates in your field; check out salary.com.
- The Freelancer's Brunch Bunch, an informal group of communications-related professionals in the Washington, D.C., metro area, offers the following tips that could be applied to just about any freelance or consulting business:

  - "Orient your resume toward specific areas in which you specialize. I have about twelve resumes specialized for technical writing—aerospace, medical, biotechnology, defense, meeting coverage, writing, teaching..." Linda Voss, science and technology writer
  - "Develop another source of income. Find something else that you're good at and find a way to make it pay. Consider branching out into a related area, such as Web site design and maintenance. For me, it was computer consulting and troubleshooting." Robert Simanski, owner, Business Pro Services
  - "Check in with current and former clients regularly; let them know that you're eager to be of service to them. Sometimes the squeaky wheel really does get the grease." David Stearman, WordMaven, Editorial Services

I also highly recommend that you join professional associations. For every career imaginable, there is an association or organization that offers a variety of resources, opportunities for training and development, and networking possibilities. A helpful book is *Weddle's Guide to Association Websites*, which includes more than 2,500 Web sites with such options as a resume database and discussion forums. The associations are organized in the book by career field and geographic location. Other resources for finding appropriate associations include:

- American Society of Association Executives, http://www.asaenet.org; click link under "networking opportunities" for ASAE's online directory
- Internet Public Libraries lists associations at http://www.ipl.org/div/aon/

JOB RESOURCES ONLINE

Many freelance and independent consulting/contracting Web sites are found under their particular field. Do an Internet search in your particular area of interest. For example, there are many writing organizations devoted to helping freelancers find work and to providing tips and ideas for surviving and thriving as a freelance writer. A good example is Washington Independent Writers, www.washwriter.org, which has a subscription-based job bank.

- www.craigslist.com, a good source for freelance work
- www.sologig.com, connecting freelancers and employers
- www.workingsolo.com

Portfolio or Flex Careers

Portfolio or flex careers are catchall terms to describe having multiple jobs in succession or at one time, including leaving, reentering, or taking a leave of absence from a career. This is becoming more and more common as job security dwindles and as people change their work habits to suit their lifestyle preferences.

Portfolio careers are a trend of the future. Career forecasters believe that before long, people working in full-time jobs will be in the minority.

Advantages of portfolio careers include:

- There is less risk of being laid off.
- Such careers offer more variety, and it can be interesting and motivating to switch gears to another job/field.
- There is less risk of boredom and frustration.
- More benefits may be available than with a more secure job.

Challenges of portfolio careers include:

- You may not have enough time to focus on one specific area.
- You don't feel connected to any single industry/field.
- You can feel scattered at times.
- You have to stay focused on the job at hand.
- You have to keep abreast of multiple fields

Tips for portfolio careers include:

- Schedule jobs very carefully to avoid overlap and burnout.
- Give yourself adequate transition time between positions.
- Try to make sure that your "bread and butter" job, the one that pays the bills, also offers benefits.
- Look for "hot" jobs or fields as a way to supplement a job or passion that doesn't make much dependable money, for example, acting, fiction writing, painting, buying and selling antiques, etc. For example:

  - Teaching. Positions are always available for adjunct professors, substitute teachers, and tutors. For substitute teaching, all that's needed is an undergraduate degree. A master's degree is preferred and sometimes required to be an adjunct or tutor, but equivalent experience in a field is often accepted. All are dependable, if rather modest, sources of income that can give you the leeway to pursue much-loved but less lucrative pursuits.

- Nursing/health care/senior care positions. There are shortages in all of these fields. Obviously, some require more training and/or education than others. It may be worth going back to school to get a nursing degree or a health-related certificate. Nurses are in such demand that they can determine their own schedule and make fairly good money working a minimal amount of time, which frees them to pursue other options.

- Internet businesses/buying and selling. This is the eBay supplement. Many people have made tidy sums operating part-time businesses online—a great option for people with "collecting" hobbies.

- Consultant/freelance work. Balance a part-time gig doing a specified number of hours as a consultant or freelancer and give yourself time to pursue your true loves and ambitions in life.

REAL-LIFE EXAMPLE: PORTFOLIO CAREER

Grace's dream was to be a runway model; however, she realized the risks and uncertainties inherent in the modeling business. To maintain her monthly income, she worked as a restaurant hostess.

We're all familiar with stories of actors and actresses who support their stage and screen dreams with restaurant tips. Who knew that the old-fashioned term "moonlighting" would one day earn the fancier moniker of "portfolio career"? The notion is that we no longer have to think of having more than one job in such stark, depressing terms. With imagination and effort, you can pursue your dreams *and* pay your bills, not just for one phase of your life but for your entire life. After all, not everyone is going to make it as a big star, but one can still have a well-balanced life with a portfolio career. And with some thought, energy, and imagination, you can think beyond waiting tables and driving taxis (not that there's anything wrong with that) and develop a more lucrative second career.

REAL-LIFE EXAMPLE: PORTFOLIO CAREER

Kate is a piano teacher with two part-time positions. In the morning she teaches music history at a university, and in the afternoon and evening she is a private piano teacher for children and adults.

For a time she worked full-time as a teacher; however, she finds her present schedule easier, more profitable, and very pleasurable. Her schedule fits her personality better. She likes the individualized attention she can give her students, and there's more variety in her daily life. She also likes getting out and seeing different parts of town rather than being stuck in the same building all day.

The greatest challenge for her at the university is that, because she's only there for a short time, she finds it difficult to get the resources and support she needs. Her personal challenge is that her vacation schedule is based on the university's schedule, and it doesn't always correspond with her family's. So she still needs to make adjustments and compromises.

All in all, though, she finds her work fun and satisfying. Music is what she loves, and she has created a lifestyle that suits her well.

Part-Time Entrepreneur

A fun, challenging, and fulfilling part-time possibility is owning, developing, and managing your own small business. Even for part-time entrepreneurs, some general rules apply. First, you must ask yourself what your goals are. Is your business idea feasible? How much money do you need to get started? Can you get the resources? Will the business be profitable?

You must create a business plan. To do this you must think through the feasibility of an idea and seek investors. Researching your potential market is essential: do people need or want your product or service? Research industry trade groups, business publications, and small business development centers for ideas on how to put a business plan together.

The key to success is to define your market as narrowly as possible. You always need to market yourself, even if you're a part-time entrepreneur. Relationship building is key. You need to keep going and establish a sense of resiliency and persistence. People who succeed are those who are comfortable promoting their business or service.

Try out your idea now; start lining up customers or clients now. Before launching my career counseling business in 1990, I designed resumes for people at night while working full-time at another job (portfolio career—see how ideas and options interconnect?). You need to be involved and highly organized. Be sensitive to your audience and willing to customize your work to their needs.

Whether you work full- or part-time as an entrepreneur, you need to be customer- and client-oriented. Focus on service, be honest and dependable. Flexibility helps. Be easy to work with and learn from others. The key to success in any business is to value existing relationships and referrals and network continuously.

Advantages of owning a part-time business:

- Independence/autonomy
- No boss
- Responsibility and decision-making power
- Keep the lion's share of financial rewards from your work
- Personal satisfaction of owning and building your own business
- Depending on the type of business, you could work out of your home, which gives you maximum flexibility in dealing with family issues (contact your local government for rules and regulations involved in running a business out of your home).

Challenges of owning a part-time business:

- You shoulder the responsibilities.

- You create support system and resources necessary to sustain business.
- You need to market continuously.
- Your profits will be uneven.
- You need to stay abreast of new developments in your field.
- Being the sole owner can lead to loneliness.

Tips on owning a part-time business:

- Do lots of market research to make sure there is a need for your product/ service.
- Have reserves in place for business downturns.
- Know your competitors.
- Network with people in your field.

RESOURCES

There are many business resources available. Here's a sampling:

- Small Business Administration, www.sba.gov
- American Business Women's Association, www.abwa.org
- American Small Businesses Association, www.asbaonline.org
- Black Business Association, www.bbala.org
- Latin Business Association, www.lbausa.com
- National Association of Women Business Owners, www.nawbo.org
- National Black Business Trade Association, www.nbbta.org
- National Business Association, www.nationalbusiness.org
- National Cooperative Business Association, www.ncba.coop
- National Small Business Association, www.nsba.biz
- Online Women's Business Center, www.onlinewbc.gov

REAL-LIFE EXAMPLE: PART-TIME CAREER COUNSELOR IN PRIVATE PRACTICE

Elin has worked four days a week since 1986. When her son was a few months old, she decided to cut her five-day-a-week position as an assistant director of continuing education at a college down to four days per week. She found the full-time schedule too draining, and she wanted to have some time to pursue her own interests: hiking, biking, and going to the gym. To make the switch, she needed to be a tough negotiator. She projected confidence that she could get the job done in the allotted time and was willing to have her salary prorated. Finally, the college agreed to her terms.

When her job ended, she started her own business as a career counselor, still working four days a week. At the time her child was two years old. Her greatest challenge is squeezing in everything that needs to be done. To make it work, she needs to be extremely efficient. This includes limiting her sessions to exactly fifty minutes, not taking a full lunch hour, and not meeting friends or colleagues for lunch.

Her greatest reward is that she feels she lives a well-balanced life.

Home-Based Business: Watch Out for Scams

Every day I receive email messages or see signs stapled to telephone poles advertising work-at-home opportunities. Some of the claims can be very seductive. Beware! If they sound too good to be true, they probably are. Don't automatically hit the reply button to proposals for envelope stuffing, craft assembly, medical billing, online businesses, and multilevel marketing opportunities (pyramid schemes) without doing your research. According to the Federal Trade Commission, those work-at-home "opportunities" are the most prevalent scams. And the problem is growing—an FBI *2004 Internet Fraud Crime Report*, available at www.fbi.gov, states that complaints related to Internet fraud, including business fraud, increased by 66 percent over 2003.

Fortunately, there are good guys and gals working the Web as well. The Federal Trade Commission (FTC), the Better Business Bureau, the FBI, and the National Consumers League offer plenty of tips and warnings for dealing with "home-based businesses."

For example, the FTC offers the following warnings in its publication, *Work-at-Home Schemes*, available online at www.ftc.gov:

- Many schemes require you to work "many hours without pay."
- Many schemes require you to "spend your own money to place newspaper ads; make photocopies; or buy the envelopes, paper, stamps, and other supplies or equipment you need to do the job."
- Many schemes require payment for instructions or necessary software.

It's best to work with a well-recognized and established company. I recommend that you visit the company if possible. If it doesn't have a real street address, watch out. I also recommend that you talk to others about their experiences in the work-at-home field.

The FTC and other organizations dedicated to warning consumers about such scams offer additional tips:

- Make sure the company is financially sound with a strong management team and proven track record. How do you do that? Start by thoroughly examining its Web site—warning signs include using free Web hosting services or free email services and having nothing but a post office box and/or no telephone number. If there is a phone number, call it and make sure it's real. Then get any printed information available—annual reports, copies of business licenses, etc. The business should also be listed in reputable business directories—contact your library for information. Contact the Better Business Bureau or your state attorney general's office to see whether complaints have been filed. Do an Internet search to see what kind of information pops up, positive or negative.
- Make sure the company actually has customers for its prod-

ucts or services, that is, will someone actually hire you to do medical billing or buy your crafts after you've paid for the start-up materials?

- Make sure there's relatively low risk involved for you—in time or money. Avoid any venture that requires significant start-up or ongoing fees. Avoid companies that promise "big profits" and "fast cash" and claim that there's little or no risk or that little or no experience is required.

- If you do invest in something, federal law requires that you receive an investor's disclosure document. If there isn't one, don't get involved.

- Ask about how and when you will be paid. Salary or commission? Who will pay you? When and how?

- If you do decide to buy something from the company, use a credit card. It is easier to track and decline payment. Know the company's refund policy.

If this all sounds too risky—perhaps you need to consider your own home-based business, rather than working for someone else's. Respond, don't react. Take your time deciding. If you're determined to get involved in the home-based business, realize that it takes time.

If you've been scammed and want to file a complaint, you can do so via:

- The Federal Trade Commission, 1-877-FTC-HELP or www. ftc.gov

- The Better Business Bureau, www.bbb.org

- The National Consumers League, www.nclnet.org, and its "Fraud Watch" organization, www.fraud.org

Home-Based Employment: Legitimate Opportunities

The best home-based opportunities evolve out of a prior job— a company that now lets you telecommute from home. Or people develop their own home-based businesses, for example, a freelance writer or graphic artist, a psychologist or career coach with a home office, business consultants, etc. Certain types of sales jobs can also be based primarily out of a home office and supplemented by time on the road. But again, people usually get these jobs through connections with a company or industry or because of significant experience in the field. This is where being a Savvy Part-Time Professional comes into play.

If you have the skills and connections, then chances are good that with moxie, vision, and creativity, you can adapt your position into a primarily work-at-home vocation. If you don't have the skills and connections, you need to get them. The best way is through experience—get a full- or part-time job in your field of interest, and once you have a base, adapt it to a work-at-home situation (see chapter 5 on how to sell this idea to employers or clients).

According to an article by Sue Shellenbarger in the *Wall Street Journal*, many large and legitimate companies—Office Depot, J. Crew, Wyndham Hotels, and Sears—are outsourcing customer-service call-answering positions to people working from their homes, as opposed to call centers domestically or abroad. According to Shellenbarger, "home-based call centers have tripled since 2000." The bad news? The pay isn't great, there usually aren't any benefits, and the work is boring and repetitive. But it is real work that you can do out of your home. People are doing it because they're desperate for flexibility. In fact, the "typical home-based call-center agent...has a college degree...and management experience."

Shellenbarger also reports that companies are looking to expand outsourcing possibilities beyond customer-service call centers. For example, sales, auditing, and underwriting have already begun using home-based workers.

As always, you need to be aware of all the pros and cons of the situation. How much are you being paid per hour, what kind of home equipment do you need (a computer and Internet access are required), whom do you report to, how are you reviewed or rated, are there opportunities for increased earnings? (See chapter 6 for a listing of outsourcing agencies.)

Direct Selling

Direct selling refers to selling performed in an arena other than a fixed retail location—think Tupperware® parties and door-to-door salesman. Of course, the market has branched out beyond that, and people directly sell everything from scrapbooks to kitchen utensils to candles to wine and more.

According to the Direct Selling Association, the industry is exploding, with approximately 50 million people involved in direct sales, and that number is growing every day. The appeal is obvious: direct selling is an ideal way to make money. As a Mary Kay spokesperson, I promoted the notion that direct selling can allow you to support your family and spend quality time with them. Direct selling gives people professional autonomy *and* a way to simplify their lives.

Advantages of direct selling include:

- You can set your own financial goals.
- Schedule appointments at your convenience.
- Work as much as you want, although your financial earnings will be in proportion to your efforts.
- According to the Direct Selling Association, you can "own a business of your own with little or no capital investment" and "receive training and support from an established company."

Challenges of direct selling include:

- This probably isn't the best option for a shy person; you need to be outgoing and aggressive.
- You stand the chance of annoying friends and relatives who may be overwhelmed by numerous invitations to "parties" and "selling events."

- You need to put in a lot of effort and sell a lot to make significant money.

Tips on direct selling include:

- Buyer beware! Do your homework. Investigate the company and verify claims. Some options are more viable than others. I recommend that you talk to others in the field and get references and recommendations. Make sure the product and business are legitimate, and the product has the potential to be profitable.
- Find a company or product you really like and believe in.
- Investigate software that makes it easier to track sales and customer and product information.
- Keep any start-up costs to a minimum.

RESOURCE
- The Direct Selling Association, http://www.dsa.org

Sales

Selling real estate, insurance, or financial services through a home-based office is often seen as a lucrative part-time opportunity. There is a demand for these fields, and companies are often willing to train you and provide a certain amount of administrative support. As with any commission-based sales position, substantial earnings are possible. However, as with any commission-based sales position, those earnings are directly tied to effort and ability.

A license is required, so you must factor in time and money investments up front. Some companies may be willing to pay for your training.

Advantages of sales include:

- Potential for high earnings.
- Support from the parent company.
- Good for high-energy, people-oriented individuals.

- Real estate can be a fun opportunity for those interested in it for investment purposes or because you like to see what other people are doing with new homes or home remodeling.

Challenges of sales include:

- These are demanding positions that are hard to work part-time. Those who are out there full-time tend to make the most money.
- Real estate and financial investment are tied to the economy, so you may have lean or slow times.
- While the work is flexible in theory, you also need to strike while the iron is hot. In other words, a client may want to see a house or sign a contract just when your son's all-star baseball tournament is scheduled.
- Often requires evening and weekend hours; need to be "on call."
- Often requires a lot of travel time, so you need a dependable car.

Tips on sales include:

- Investigate both the field and the various companies thoroughly to see which one offers the best deal in terms of money-making potential, training, administrative support, etc.
- Talk regularly to others in the field: network, network, network.
- Examine your interests, values, and personality type (see chapter 3) to help determine whether this type of sales position is a good match for you.

Flex-Leaves and Sabbaticals

The Family and Medical Leave Act (FMLA) guarantees mothers and fathers twelve weeks of unpaid leave to care for children, whether biological or adopted, provided they have worked at least 1,250 hours for an employer with more than fifty employees. Of course, this stipulation leaves many without such a guarantee. According to the Families and Work Institute, the U.S. Department of Labor cites that only 47 percent of employees meet FMLA requirements.

Make sure you understand what your company offers regarding flex-leaves and sabbaticals. Read the company manual and speak with the human resources department.

A sabbatical is when you arrange with your employer to take time off, paid or unpaid, for personal reasons. You can take a long vacation, pursue an interest, further your training or development, take care of a child, or simply take a long break because you need one. A sabbatical is a great opportunity to refresh and reenergize yourself. It can also be a growth opportunity if you choose to pursue a new interest.

Many organizations require employees to have completed one year's service to be considered for a sabbatical. Contractual agreements vary, although there is no legal requirement to keep the job open. According to the advocacy group, Working Families, sometimes an employee is required to resign before taking a sabbatical, with the idea that he or she will be strongly considered for employment upon return. Nothing is guaranteed in this situation, however.

According to a recent study by the Society for Human Resource Management (www.shrm.org), only 4 percent of employers polled offer paid sabbaticals, while about 17 percent offer unpaid ones. It's unlikely that your sabbatical will be paid by the organization, although a few dynamic companies invest in what can be a win-win situation for both the company and the employee. Sometimes a sabbatical is offered to recognize loyalty and commitment; sometimes it's offered as a way to keep hard-charging professionals from burning out. The academic community often offers sabbaticals as a way for instructors to pursue research, fieldwork, or additional degrees.

Though it's unlikely that a sabbatical will be paid, at more creative companies sabbaticals are becoming increasingly in vogue. According to a recent *Wall Street Journal* article, "Sabbaticals: The Pause that Refreshes," "publishing, high technology, advertising and consulting companies" have recently instituted sabbaticals in the belief that if you don't give employees time to regenerate or recharge, they will burn out. The article cited Bertelsmann, the publishing arm of AG's Random House, which recently began a paid sabbatical program for older employees. According to chief executive Peter Olson, "The company estimates that more than 800 of its nearly 3,000 employees in the U.S., including editors, warehouse workers, and salespeople will take a sabbatical by the end of 2006." To qualify, an employee has to have been with the company for at least ten years. According to Olson, although the idea of sabbaticals was initially met with resistance, he went ahead anyway because the advantages "outweigh the downside of the additional work for managers."

According to Charlotte and Laura Shelton in their book, *The Next Revolution—What Gen X Women Want at Work and How Their Boomer Bosses Can Help Them Get It*, Deloitte & Touche launched a program, called "Personal Pursuits," that lets above-average performers take up to five years off. To keep employees engaged in the field, the company pays for professional licensing fees and weeklong annual training sessions.

I believe companies need to offer sabbaticals as they would any other benefit. Many clients I have worked with who were going through difficult, uncertain times would have greatly appreciated this option if it had been available to them. Instead, many of them had to leave their positions. Both these employees and their companies could have derived value if the individuals had been allowed a break to recharge. It is expensive to hire a new employee, and the time needed to get a new hire up to speed is considerable. A brief break can allow a stressed-out employee to gain perspective and return with a new attitude and a desire to work.

Besides the cost, one disadvantage to a sabbatical is that

you may find the return to work to be a hard transition. After being away, it can be difficult to reengage. At present, there are no particular laws regarding sabbaticals.

Advantages of a sabbatical include:

- Serves as a motivator and reward to talented employees.
- Refreshes and regenerates.
- Retains employees who would have left due to burnout.
- Cross-trains other employees who need to pick up slack.
- Broadens one's horizons depending on how the time is spent.
- Helps in developing skills.

Challenges of a sabbatical include:

- Makes additional work for managers.
- Forces other employees to pick up the slack.
- The returning employee needs to ease back into his or her job.
- Other employees might resent the returning employee.

Tips for a sabbatical include:

- Plan ahead and make necessary adjustments on leaving and returning to work.

Seasonal Work

When you work on a seasonal basis, you usually work full-time for a portion of the year with time off during the remaining months. This term usually conjures up images of high school and college students or surfing "bums" looking to finance their next adventure. That's all true, but seasonal work also offers opportunities for professionals.

As many of these opportunities (not all!) involve relocating for part of the year, this lifestyle is best suited to the adventurous and the footloose and fancy-free. The tourism and recreation fields offer the lion's share of seasonal employment opportunities. Guides are needed to lead everything from adventure outings to history or art tours. Parks—local, state, and national—need seasonal employees. Camps for adults, teens, and children all require professional adult staff—not just recreation leaders, but administrators and medical staff as well. Many resorts (and cruise ships) employ seasonal professionals, including medical staff, administrators, massage therapists, exercise instructors, skin care technicians, and entertainers. In addition, many resorts now offer nutrition classes and counseling services, thus expanding their employee pools to include nutritionists, psychologists, and other professionals. If you have the flexibility, you can live and work in some of the most beautiful spots in the world.

The education field offers professional seasonal employment opportunities locally, nationally, and internationally via summer school, work abroad programs, and tutoring sessions (SAT prep, etc.)

Some industries operate only a portion of the year. If you're truly adventurous, you can earn big money fishing or crabbing in Alaska. Keep in mind that some of these jobs are dangerous; don't do this on a lark—know what you're getting into.

Those in health care are really limited only by their imagination in terms of the jobs they could get for a portion of the year. Many exciting travel opportunities are available, but a health care professional could just as easily arrange to work a portion of the year from home—hospitals, at-home services, and elder care facilities are all hungry for employees and are often willing to work with you in setting up a schedule.

Those in the medical and educational fields aren't the only ones who can arrange seasonal work from their home base. Accountants can work only during the tax season, and retail provides opportunities for working during holiday or other "high" seasons. Airports may be looking to supplement their workforces during their busy seasons. Investigate security-related jobs, which also offer opportunities for part-time or seasonal work.

Advantages of seasonal work include:

- Lots of time every year to pursue your interests in the off-season.
- A chance to participate in rewarding activities in exciting locations.
- If you're restless by nature, the variety of experiences and time off can keep you from burning out and getting bored.
- A great way to experiment with different career choices or locations.
- Great for seniors who don't have the family obligations, who often live in two locations (think snowbirds), and who have additional retirement money and benefits to cover them in the off–season.
- Great for singles—a great way to meet people, get out in the world, and have wonderful adventures.

Challenges of seasonal work include:

- Budgeting money to last during the off-season.
- There often are no benefits, unless you're in a high-need field such as nursing.
- Difficult for people with children who need stability.

Tips for seasonal work include:

- Budget carefully.
- Make sure you have insurance (see chapter 11).
- Sublet your apartment/house if you can.
- Investigate a home-trade for the season.

RESOURCES
Job search sites come and go, and some are better than others. While I can't vouch for the quality of the following, here are

some sites to start your search:

- www.backdoorjobs.com
- www.coolworks.com
- www.ecojobs.com
- www.greatcampjobs.com
- www.jobmonkey.com
- www.quintcareers.com; has links to many other sites.
- www.seasonalemployment.com
- Information on temporary positions and seasonal employment with the National Park Service, www.sep.nps.gov
- www.summerjobs.com

REAL-LIFE EXAMPLE: SEMI-SEASONAL EMPLOYMENT: TAX ACCOUNTANT

Amy, an accountant, has a dual residency; she has a house in Italy along with a small accounting practice and an apartment in New York, where she works as an accountant during the tax season. Italy is her preferred residence because it's less stressful, and she returns there three to four times a year.

The greatest challenge for her is developing relationships in both places and balancing her personal life. She enjoys her work, which is particularly intense during the two-month tax season. She also appreciates the professional freedom of working at her own pace and being her own boss. Amy has made financial sacrifices; for example, to have more clients, she would need to spend more time in the United States, which is not something she's willing to do because she enjoys her life in Italy.

Travel is important to her, and her life is set up for traveling throughout Europe. I would describe her as someone with an adventurous spirit. At twenty, she wanted to speak another language and work in an embassy, and that's exactly what she did. She makes things happen. She believes in taking risks and, obviously, she has taken many in her life. Amy believes that if you know what you really want, you can achieve anything. All of her choices reflect her belief in living life to its fullest and that is exactly what she has done.

Temporary or "Temp" Positions

Working for a temp agency is usually thought of as a transitional position for those seeking full-time work, and it can be a good way for someone to get their foot in the door of a company. However, some people choose this route so they can have the utmost in flexibility. The scheduling possibilities are wide open. Some people use temp agencies to work only part of the year, part of the week, or part-time on a daily basis.

Many of these positions are administrative, but not all. There are temp agencies for attorneys, for example. Some of the administrative-type positions can be fun and educational, such as staffing conferences and workshops. In addition to getting paid for part-time work, you can basically sit in on the conference, lecture, or workshop free of charge. Working conferences or trade shows is also a great way to network and meet interesting people.

If you work a certain number of hours, you may qualify for sick leave and vacation benefits.

Advantages of working as a "temp" include:

- Set your own schedule. You pick your days, availability, location (commuting limits).
- Good for those who like variety.
- Opportunity to learn new skills, network, and get an inside look at different companies and fields of interest. (Remember my recommendation to "try out" an experience before committing? This is a good way to do it.)
- Temps who prove their worth are often offered permanent part- or full-time positions.
- You don't have to do the marketing or job search, and you incur no overhead costs.

Challenges of working as a "temp" include:

- If you're only there for a couple of days, people sometimes treat you as if you're invisible.
- Stepping into an unknown situation can be scary and anxiety-provoking. You need to adapt quickly and think on your feet.
- Tend to get the "boring" jobs that no one else wants to do.
- You may not get the job or company you want, when you want it.
- Inconsistent pay.

Tips on working as a "temp":

- It's a good idea to establish yourself with one temp agency. It gets to know and depend on you. You'll get the better assignments, and your pay will increase as you build experience and a track record.
- Be self-sufficient. You may end up working at the same company or round of companies on a temp basis, or you may job jump. Be prepared for all contingencies: pack your own lunch and snacks and carry a briefcase with life's necessities—tissues, water, cell phone, toothbrush, change for vending machines, anything to help ease you through your day.
- Overdress on the first day, then adapt to the dress code of the office.
- If it's a new assignment, allow yourself plenty of commuting time to get to a new location.
- Develop a specialty or niche, and you'll get more money: experience in certain software programs, IT troubleshooting, etc.

RESOURCES
- www.corestaff.com
- www.kellyservices.com (way back when, this used to be

known as "Kelly Girls")
- www.manpower.com
- www.olsten.com
- www.net-temps.com
- www.temping.com
- www.weststaff.com

RESOURCES

- www.eeoc.gov (information about enforcement of federal anti-discrimination laws)
- www.irs.gov (information about independent contractor status)
- www.dol.gov (information about Family and Medical Leave Act and federal wage and hour laws; includes links to state Web sites)
- www.findlaw.com/employment (general information for employees and employers about federal and state laws affecting employment, including unemployment insurance and workers' compensation)
- www.ssa.gov/publications (electronic leaflet, *How Work Affects Your Benefits*)

Employment Rights of Part-Time Employees

Judith Moldover, counsel to the law firm of Ford & Harrison, discusses the employment rights of part-time employees, consultants, and temporary employees:

Everyone understands that forty hours is the standard workweek for full-time work in the U.S. Few people realize that there is no definition, legal or otherwise, of part-time work that applies to all employees in all workplaces. Each employer is free to determine whether part-time work is permitted and, if so, whether there are minimum or maximum hours for part-time workers. This freedom may be limited by a collective bargaining agreement restricting part-time or temporary employment of union-represented employees.

If you are a regular part-time employee, you have many of the same basic legal rights as a full-time employee. For instance, you have the same protections as your employer's full-time employees when it comes to laws prohibiting race, sex, age, disability, and other types of discrimination. You also have the same protections under laws regulating wages and hours, military leave, and occupational safety and health. Remember that if, like many part-time workers, you are paid by the hour rather than on fixed salary, you will be eligible for overtime pay in any week in which you work more than 40 hours, even though you perform professional work. Eligibility for unemployment compensation and workers' compensation is governed by state law and may include part-time workers.

When it comes to most employee benefits, however, part-timers have few legal rights. In the U.S., employers are not legally required to give paid vacation, sick days, holidays, or severance. Many employers who do give them to full-time employees withhold them from part-time employees. There is a growing trend, however, to offer pro-rated benefits to part-timers. Included in this trend is offering medical benefits to regular part-time employees who work a minimum number of hours, usually at least

20 hours per week. A federal law mandates that an employee who works at least 1,000 hours in a plan-specified 12-month period may participate in the employer's pension plans, including any 401(k) plan, provided the employee is not part of an excluded class of employees. Another federal law, the Family and Medical Leave Act, provides job protection during medical or maternity/paternity leave for employees of covered employers who have worked at least 1,250 hours in the 12 months prior to the leave, as long as they have worked for that employer for at least 12 months, which need not be consecutive. You can become eligible by working any schedule that results in 1,250 hours in a 12-month period (for instance, by working 25 hours a week for 50 weeks). Some states have their own version of this law, and may have different requirements.

Retirees considering part-time work for the same employer from which they retired must check with the benefits department to see if this work will have any effect on their pension payments. It is legal for a pension plan to suspend, or even to permanently withhold, payments if the retiree works more than 40 hours in any month, although not all plans choose to do this. If you work before reaching full retirement age (65 years and 6 months in 2005), Social Security payments may be reduced if your earnings exceed a certain dollar amount; currently there is no reduction in payments after full retirement age no matter how much you earn.

If you are a part-time consultant, you are not an employee at all. Most legal rights you have will come from your agreement with your client. You should have a written agreement because oral agreements are not enforceable in court in most states if they cannot be performed in one year. A signed letter or series of letters can create an enforceable contract, but it is usually better to have a formal agreement. Consultants may legally be eligible to participate in a client's executive compensation plans, but the client's plan design determines the extent of participation, if any. To be a true consultant (i.e., an independent contractor), you

Continued from Page 91

must run your own business with no client input into how you accomplish your results. There are various tests to determine independent contractor status under federal law. If your client classifies you as a consultant but in reality you are a part-time employee, your "client" is subject to penalties by federal, state, and local taxing authorities for failing to withhold employment taxes. You may also be eligible for any employee benefits and wages which you should have received as a part-time employee.

If you are a full-time temporary employee, your rights depend on how you are employed. If you work through a temporary agency, you are the agency's employee. In some situations, you may be considered to be jointly employed by both the temporary agency and its client. If you are employed directly as a temporary full-time employee, you will have many of the same rights, or lack thereof, as a part-time employee. Because a full-time "temp" who works for one employer continually over a long period may be entitled to the same employment benefits as a regular full-time employee, some companies limit the length of time during which they will employ any one individual as a "temp."

CHAPTER 5

How to Sell Your Proposal to Your Employer and Negotiate the Best Package

Some of the most successful arrangements for part-time work come about when people adapt their full-time position to a part-time or flexible work arrangement. Why? Because an employer who knows your worth often is willing to pay you an equivalent salary and maintain your benefits (prorated) in exchange for keeping you and your knowledge and skill sets within the company.

It's harder to find a "new" job in which people are willing to accommodate your schedule and needs before they get to know you. In that case, you could start a full-time position with the goal of converting it to part-time once you've proven your worth to your employer.

Do Your Homework

Before you approach your employer with a proposal for a part-time or any other flexwork schedule, do your research. Does your company already have a policy on part-time work, job sharing, telework, or flextime? Don't overlook this step; it's critical that you understand policies and why such situations have succeeded or failed. If the company doesn't have a system in place, don't despair. Yours could be the first.

You also need to be well versed in your arguments about why this change is a good idea for your employer, and you need to know what the objections might be so you can counter them.

Eventually, you will write up your request in proposal form, give it to your employer to read and digest, and then set up a time to discuss it. I go over all these steps in detail. Depending on your situation, however, you may want to float the idea by your manager first so he or she won't feel blindsided when the proposal suddenly appears. If you have a fairly friendly and open relationship with management, this is the way to go. On the other hand, if you're in a highly structured, rather "cold" environment or if you have to go through a human resources department or committee, you may want to wait until you can deliver a well-thought-out plan in writing.

Before you get to that step—writing a proposal and presenting it—you need to start brainstorming and researching.

- Determine how flexible your position is. Be realistic but also be creative. Some positions such as computer-based jobs are easily adaptable; others that require working with the public during set hours present more of a challenge. In these cases, you may want to consider job sharing.
- Write down your ideal situation, but be ready to compromise. List what you need and want in your personal order of priority. This is personal information for your eyes only to help you determine what is most and least important to you. Remember, your employer is only really going to want to know what's in it for him or her (though keeping employees happy is also an argument).
- Write down what your employer needs from you. Put each of these obligations under a microscope to see how it could be adapted to part-time or flextime. Consider how this will affect your work with clients and co-workers. Will it cost the company money or extra time to implement this position and keep track of it? How will the success of the new position and your performance be evaluated? What possible problems may arise from working on this proposed schedule? Be creative and think of any and all problems so you'll be able to have an answer or solution ready to counter each one.

- Find someone else or, better yet, several people who are successfully employed part-time and get tips and ideas on working reduced hours. Seek out those people in fields and positions similar to yours and talk to them about every aspect of the job, including how they got it. If possible, speak with people who have *negotiated* part-time positions. In addition, read all the "real-life examples" in this book for further inspiration and information.

  Certain fields have associations or advocacy/resource centers devoted to part-time or flextime professionals, including the Association of Part-time Librarians (http://www2.canisius.edu/ ~ huberman/aptl.html) and the Project for Attorney Retention, which, according to its Web site, www.pardc.org, "seeks to improve recruiting and retention of talented attorneys through the use of work schedules that allow attorneys to better balance the competing demands of their work and their lives outside the office." These are examples of great sites to get specific ideas and tips for your field and to chat with colleagues.

- List the advantages to your employer of a part-time situation (see Selling the Advantages to Your Employer in this chapter).

- Brainstorm your employer's possible objections and prepare a counterargument (see Be Prepared for Common Employer Objections in this chapter).

- Prepare to market yourself to your employer. Know your value to the company and list your accomplishments.

- Think all the details through. For example, if you plan to telecommute from home, let your employer know what you're willing to do or have done to prepare. Give your employer a detailed list of how you plan to equip your office—computer, fax, etc. Know the costs you will incur and what you might be saving your employer and see if you can negotiate to have your employer pay for a computer, extra phone lines, computer support, etc. (see Proposal Tips for Telework in this chapter.)

- Know your bottom line in terms of salary and go for benefits. Part-time employees have historically been paid less and have been cut out of benefits, though this is changing as more and more professionals seek this option and use their well-honed skills and experience to leverage better compensation packages (see Negotiating Compensation in this chapter).

- Have a backup plan in case your employer refuses to accept your proposal. What are your options? Are you prepared to quit and seek a new position elsewhere? If you can't reduce your hours, maybe you can arrange to work out of your home (telework) once or twice a week. Or maybe you can negotiate flexible arrival/departure times or flexible lunch hours. Don't threaten your employer with "I'll quit if I don't get what I want." Keep it positive and aim for a win-win during negotiations. But you should know in advance what steps you're prepared to take. Any time you enter a negotiation, you should know what you must have, what you're willing to give up, and what your backup plan is if all fails.

- Timing is everything. Time the presentation of your part-time proposal. If you're company is really in a desperate crunch or facing a deadline, this may seem like the perfect time to make your pitch. Be aware, however, that you may cause bad feelings by exerting pressure when your boss is under the gun. You may get the job in the short run, but the ill will you create may cost you. It's also not a good idea to wait until the company is sitting fat and happy, thinking it has all the time in the world to look for your replacement. Go for the "in-between" time, if there ever is one in your field. Think of it as the calm before the storm of a not-so-distant deadline. Your employer won't be overly stressed, but neither will he or she have a lot of time to train someone when he or she has a highly qualified person in you.

- Once you have an agreed-on proposal, get an agreement in writing so both you and your boss have a written point of reference.

Selling the Advantages to Your Employer: A Win-Win Situation for All

This is the key part of your proposal. Most people want to know what's in it for them. Create tangible reasons why this can make sense for your employer. It's about working smart—not solely working long hours. It is also possible to let your employer know that he or she can try out a situation on a trial basis to see how it will work for both of you.

There have been numerous studies over the years demonstrating the advantages of workplace flexibility to employers and employees. Some key findings from those studies and other sources include:

- Increased ability to *attract, motivate, and retain* high-performing and experienced employees. Research shows that high-quality professionals of all ages—Generation Xers, parents, baby boomers, seniors—are seeking to balance life and work. To attract and keep experienced, creative, top-quality staff, employers have to get creative with their work schedule policies.

  The Project for Attorney Retention (PAR) reports that one Washington, D.C., law firm has created a "Balanced Hours Program" for part-time attorneys. According to PAR, the "balanced hours allow firms to attract and retain top legal talent, which is essential to good service. More importantly, balanced hours programs recognize the need to address client dissatisfaction with turnover in their outside counsel."

  Another study reported that the turnover rate for half-time workers was 14 percent, compared to an average of 40 percent for full-time workers (*The Job/Family Challenge* by Ellen Bravo; cited in *Breaking with Tradition* by Felice Schwartz).

  The Families and Work Institute reports that in a 1998 survey, half the companies ranked flexibility as the best retention tool over salaries, stock options, and training.

- Turnover is very expensive. You're a skilled, experienced worker. The cost of hiring and training someone to replace you—someone who is an unknown quantity at this point—can be very daunting. Your part-time proposal is at least worth a try on this point alone. The Families and Work Institute's *When Work Works* project reports that "The Saratoga Institute found it costs 150 to 200 percent of an exempt person's yearly salary to replace him or her."

  In a *Wall Street Journal* article by Loretta Chao, "For Gen Xers, It's Work to Live," Richard Lamond, chief of human resources for a Florida staffing firm, says "one accepted method for calculating the cost of losing an employee—including the expense of recruiting, relocating and training a replacement—is to multiply the salary by 1.5. The average salary for a white-collar worker in the U.S. in 2004 was $42,000, according to the Department of Labor, so replacing a departing worker could cost an employer around $63,000."

- Reduced absenteeism. People are able to take care of pressing personal matters on their own time without taking off work. A less hectic schedule also pays off in reduced absenteeism.

- Enhanced productivity. Part-time employees are more focused at work because they need to get their work done within a specified time. Studies have shown that half-time workers were, on average, 89 percent as productive as full-time employees, *in half the time!* In other words, the half-time workers produced nearly nine-tenths of the work of their full-time counterparts in half the time (*Breaking with Tradition* by Felice Schwartz).

- Saves employers money. With your enhanced productivity, you'll actually save your employer money in salary and benefits. Be careful with this one though—your employer may try to squeeze a full-time job into a part-time job. Even if he or she has to hire another part-time person to round out the position—he or she will still save with both of you working at enhanced levels of productivity.

- Increased employee job satisfaction, motivation, creativity, and ability to handle stress translate into improved worker output.

FURTHER RESOURCES

See *When Work Works*, available online at the Families and Work Institute's Web site, www.familiesandwork.org, for more study and data ammunition to bolster your case.

My Observations for Increased Worker Efficiency

My experience with clients over the years bears out the fact that workers who feel that their work/life needs are understood and balanced are more productive. Whenever a client of mine is working in a situation where there is little camaraderie and understanding between that person and his or her boss, stress and dissatisfaction result. Everyone appreciates a boss who treats him or her with respect, kindness, and dignity. As a result, the employee is more willing to pitch in when needed and is more focused and interested in his or her work.

For example, it's been shown that managers who work with their employees in a partnership/coaching model achieve better results than do those who work in an authoritarian model. The employee's and employer's goals are more in line with one another, which leads to increased productivity and profitability.

I have also observed that part-time professionals are very focused when at work. What do I mean by that? When working part-time, you have to make the most of your hours in the office; there is very little slack time. Part-time professionals know how to set priorities, as they have little wiggle room. Part-time employees also don't take as much time off for personal reasons or spend as much time on the phone taking care of personal matters.

While I was working in a corporation, I observed that one day a week is probably lost due to poor time management and lack of focus on the part of full-time employees. I did an informal study of managers and employees, and they confirmed this. It's very difficult to be fully productive eight-plus hours a day for five consecutive days.

Be Prepared for Common Employer Objections

You need to be prepared for possible objections to your proposed job arrangement, and you need to be ready to respond clearly and confidently with counterarguments. Here's a list of common objections with possible responses:

- *Employer:* We've never done this before.

  Response: Perhaps we can give it a trial run so you can see that it works, and then we can reassess the situation in three months' time.
- *Employer:* This job can't be done part-time.

  Response: I disagree. I've divided the job into clear responsibilities, and I believe with proper organization and time management skills it can be done. Regarding client contact, I will do my best in my part-time arrangement to be in close contact with our clients, and in extreme circumstances, I will make myself available to clients during nonwork hours. (Here's where you turn to your list of anticipated problems so you can be very specific about your particular position.)
- *Employer:* Other employees will resent what they see as their increased workload.

  Response: I've given careful thought to the days I'll work part-time to minimize any conflicts. I also plan to communicate very clearly with all staff and give sufficient notice regarding deadlines and projects and how to find and retrieve information. I have clear communication guides for when, where, and how I can be reached. As a matter of fact, I believe this arrangement can help my colleagues to become more time-sensitive and results-oriented. I plan to monitor the situation and solicit regular feedback to make sure no one feels overburdened. I'll also be careful not to gloat about the new situation.

- *Employer:* Everyone will want to do this.

  Response: Some people might, and that's not a bad situation because it will allow you, the employer, to attract and retain top-notch, hardworking personnel. However, most people still need to work full-time for the extra salary and benefits, and others want to work full-time for the social support and structure.

Proposal: Putting It on Paper

Keep it clean and simple. Use lots of bullet points or put it in a chart, but make sure you document your information; if you quote a study, for example, say which study and where to find it. Chances are your employer won't look it up, but it adds weight.

I've given you some general ideas for your proposal in the preceding sections—advantages to employers, possible objections, the benefits of work/life balance, etc. Here are some tips for specific situations, such as proposed job shares, telework, and sabbaticals.

Further Negotiating Tips for Specific Situations

JOB SHARES

- In the job description section of the proposal, be very specific about how you will split up the duties.
- Communication is key. Employers/supervisors often worry about the continuity of communication between staff/customers and those in a job share. Be prepared to answer:

  - Who will communicate with customers and clients?
  - How will both partners communicate?
  - How will job share partners communicate with internal staff?
  - Who will attend meetings?

- Emphasize advantages to the employer. Treat it as a win-

win situation for both you and the organization, but keep the focus on why this is good for the company.

- Job shares help retain and attract high-quality employees.
- Clients and staff have consistent access to a responsible person.
- Employer gains two sets of skills for one job.
- The position is always covered—no gaps for vacation/sick days/personal days.

● Have ideas for evaluation of the position. For example, what happens if one person falls behind in his or her work? What happens if one person outperforms the other? Will salaries always be equal? How will opportunities for promotions/training be handled?

● Have a contingency plan if one person leaves the position. What happens to the other job share person? Is that person willing to work full-time until a replacement is found? Treat this as a built-in advantage for the employer. After all, full-time people also leave positions, which often leaves a position totally uncovered. At least this way, a position would be covered part-time until a replacement is found (and according to studies, many people out there would love a job share).

● Research others who have been successful and share their stories.

● If you and your job share partner don't need health benefits because you're both covered by a spouse, that would save the company money. But don't be too quick to give up benefits. Try to get everything you can get.

● Offer a trial period if your employer is uncertain.

FURTHER RESOURCES

● The government of Manitoba, Canada, has a helpful online guide to job sharing, including job sharing arrangements, tips, and ideas for proposals, http://www.gov.mb.ca/csc/publications/jbsharguid.html

- The federal government's Office of Personnel Management also has a very good *Part-Time Employment and Job Sharing Guide,* http://www.opm.gov/Employment_and_Benefits/ WorkLife/OfficialDocuments/handbooksguides/ PT_Employ_JobSharing/pt08.asp
- http://workoptions.com/jobshare.htm has free tips and resources and sells templates for proposals for various flexwork jobs, including job shares

Sabbaticals

If your employer doesn't offer sabbaticals, think about proposing one. Make it a win-win situation. Research and talk with others who have taken a sabbatical and ask them what they thought the costs and benefits were for both their companies and for themselves. Let your employer know very clearly how it will benefit him or her. For example, if you're getting additional training or education, emphasize that; a better-trained employee is an advantage to the company in the long run.

Perhaps more important, sabbaticals often rank as a favorite employee benefit. They're a great way to attract and hold on to bright, creative, experienced employees. As such, more and more companies, from accounting to law firms to financial institutions, are offering sabbaticals as a way to avoid burnout among their hard-charging pros.

I know a woman who worked at a nonprofit organization, where it was typical practice for each employee to take a month off during the summer to travel and/or pursue an interest. She and her colleagues came back rejuvenated and refreshed, thus benefiting the company as well as its employees.

Though sabbaticals are catching on in other areas, they are still most typical in academia. A nationwide survey of community college administrators, "Sabbatical as a Form of Faculty Renewal in the Community College" (www.eric.ed.gov), explored the purposes, benefits, and outcomes of sabbatical leaves. Key findings include:

- More than half of the colleges surveyed offered sabbatical programs.
- Most administrators reported that faculty who participated in the programs felt "professionally enriched," "rejuvenated," or "updated."
- Two-thirds of the respondents said that improved teaching was the primary desired outcome of their college's sabbatical program.

Be prepared to counter common objections, such as, who will fill in for you while you're gone? Some of these don't have easy answers—you're going to have to put some time into analyzing your particular position and company. For example, if you and your colleagues can take turns taking sabbaticals, then everyone is much more amenable to picking up the slack for an employee on leave.

Keep in mind that sabbaticals are often seen as a reward for outstanding work, so emphasize your service to the company and your future value.

Proposal Tips for Telework

Telework (more and more experts prefer this term as it sounds more beneficial to the employer), or telecommuting, seems to grow in popularity as more traffic congestion and higher gas prices, combined with advances in technology, make working from home an efficient option. You know why it's good for you, but remember, always emphasize what's in it for your employer. As with many of the best part-time or flexible positions, this works best when you're a proven employee asking for a conversion to telework.

Advantages to emphasize include:

- Lower overhead for the employer. According to the Canadian Telework Association, "your organization could save 1 office for every 3 teleworkers (that's about $2,000 per teleworker per year, or $200,000 per 100 teleworkers)."

- No commuting time. Employees can work at their peak personal functioning times without the stress, frustration, costs, and wasted time involved in commuting.
- A very appealing recruitment and retention tool. Via telework, employers can also hang on to valuable employees who relocate.
- Enhanced productivity. Check the telework associations listed in the resource section for examples of the many studies that document increased productivity. Make sure you include a cost/benefit analysis in your proposal. This type of "homework" pays off in the long run.
- Fewer sick days for personal reasons, weather, etc.
- You could always propose a "try-out" period.

Possible objections from your employer include:

- Interruptions due to caregiving responsibilities. Most employers know whether you have babies, children, or sick or elderly relatives to care for at home, so be sure to address your plan for dealing with this situation during working hours, for example, you have hired in-house care, your children are in school/day care for part of the day, etc.
- Fear of goofing off. It's human nature to think that while the cat's away, the mice will play, so you need to have a system of accountability for while you're at home working. For example, you'll check in with emails or phone calls at regular intervals. Remember, many computer-based communication systems can show when you're "idle" at your computer.

  This is also a situation where time will tell. Make sure you're producing at an above-average level, especially at the beginning of your telework experience. However don't overproduce on a level that will be impossible to maintain over the long haul or you'll burn out. Make sure you and your boss have realistic expectations.
- Communication issues. Make sure that your supervisor, co-

workers, and clients always know how to reach you during work hours. Be prepared to wear your cell phone on your belt. Invest in a phone headset that gives you mobility around the house and in your car.

A key item to think about and negotiate is home office operating expenses. Who is going to pay for the computer, fax, extra phone line, phone bills, etc., and who is going to arrange and pay for repairs caused by the inevitable computer breakdowns and problems? This can get a little tricky and depends on your personal situation. If you're in sales or marketing and bring income into your company in a very direct way, you probably stand the best chance of getting the company to pay for everything. Highly experienced and valued employees likewise stand a better chance.

If you and your company are relatively new to telework, you may need to pay more of the expenses up-front or work out a shared arrangement. For example, you pay for the computer/phone/fax equipment since it doubles for home use, and your employer pays for the extra fax or phone line and computer repairs. After you've secured the telework agreement and proven it to be successful, you can always renegotiate.

You must know, however, whom you're going to call when you encounter the inevitable computer problems, and who is going to pay for it. I strongly advise that you use the company's troubleshooter and negotiate hard for the company to pay for it—because the cost in lost work time will damage your company, and repairs will damage your pocketbook. Remember, that computers break down at the office as well, so don't let this be a sticking point for management.

Also, be aware that telecommuters may face new taxes. This needs to be taken into account when negotiating. According to an article in the *Wall Street Journal*, "Telecommuters May Face New Taxes on Their Income," in late 2005 the Supreme Court "declined to hear an appeal by a Tennessee man who telecommuted to New York and was charged by that state for taxes on all his income." This means teleworkers may have to deal with higher state income tax bills if other states follow suit. However, according to the article, "members of Congress already have introduced legislation to protect telecommuters from such taxes."

FURTHER RESOURCES

- The American Telecommuting Association, http://www.knowledgetree.com/ata.html
- Canadian Telework Association, http://www.ivc.ca/
- International Telework Association & Council, www.workingfromanywhere.org
- The Telework Coalition, www.telcoa.org
- Washington Metropolitan Area Telework Centers, www.wmtc.org; although this is a regional site, it has good information on the benefits of telework, including a "savings calculator" to help you figure out how much gas money you'll save and the amount of pollution you'll reduce by telecommuting. Check your particular region for local telework organizations or advisory councils; using an Internet search engine, type in your state's name, along with "telework" or "telecommuting," to see what's available.
- Working Moms Refuge Web site, www.momsrefuge.com/telecommute/resources/index.html, has a list

Telework Proposal Template

JOB DESCRIPTION SUMMARY

Here's an outline to get your started on your proposal. Use the information from this chapter and specific information related to your job.

Describe your job in major and minor responsibilities and what can be done in and outside the office.

- Major responsibilities
- Minor responsibilities

- Office-based responsibilities
- Home-based office responsibilities

HIGHLIGHT YOUR ACCOMPLISHMENTS/ VALUE AS AN EMPLOYEE

Advantages to employer include:

- Productivity enhancement. Use the information in this chapter to address how productivity is generally enhanced by teleworking, for example, you can work without constant office distractions. Then get as specific to your job as possible.
- Cost/benefits analysis to employer, for example, no office space costs, reduced absenteeism, and better retention means less money spent on finding and training your replacement.
- Happier employees equals motivated and loyal employees.

PROPOSED SCHEDULE

Days and hours you will work from home and from the office. Will it be a set schedule or will you be able to have some flexibility?

PROPOSED COMMUNICATION SCHEDULE WITH CLIENTS/COLLEAGUES

- List hours you are available for contact via phone, fax, and computer.
- Address how you will meet deadlines and how often you will attend meetings, conferences, etc. Will you attend meetings by phone?
- Describe how you will let the office know where all your information is kept and how to access it. Don't be afraid to detail the obvious, for example, "all email addresses are in my online email address book or Rolodex®."

EQUIPMENT COSTS

List equipment you have on hand and other equipment you will need.

STRATEGY TO EVALUATE SUCCESS OF FLEXIBLE POSITION
To be reviewed in three months' time.

EVALUATION OF POSITION
Will be evaluated on performance with clear measurable results that are mutually decided on, in six months' time.

PRESENTATION POINTS TO KEEP IN MIND
You need to propose your situation in person. Be prepared to counter objections, focus on the benefits to the company, and highlight your accomplishments and achievements. Be professional and prepared to negotiate. Good luck!

FURTHER RESOURCES FOR PREPARING A PROPOSAL
You can view other examples of flexible work arrangement templates and example proposals and agreements at:

- Duke Human Resources, http://www.hr.duke.edu/flexwork/faq.html
- Flexwork, http://www.flexwork.eu.com/map.html
- Microsoft Office Online, http://office.microsoft.com/en-us/FX012074031033.aspx
- University of Michigan, http://www.umich.edu/ ~ hraa/worklife/docs/sampleflex.pdf
- www.workingfamilies.org.uk; this is a British Web site, but it has a free interactive guide to "preparing your proposal for flexible working" (click on the "family zone" link, and then the "online guide to flexible working")
- www.workoptions.com; for a fee, you can purchase a comprehensive proposal template for telecommuting, part-time, job sharing, or a compressed workweek (this site also includes free tips and resources)

Tips for Negotiating Compensation

Once you've convinced your employer to consider a reduced-hours arrangement, you can focus on pay and benefits. To be a truly Savvy Part-Time Professional, you have to be paid what you're worth. It comes down to being prepared by doing your research, knowing your worth to the company and within the marketplace, knowing your priorities and values, understanding benefits and knowing which ones you need and want, and then demonstrating the self-worth, self-esteem, and guts to find and negotiate the right position and package.

First, you need to know your worth—in terms of both the general pay scale for your line of work and position and your individual worth to your company. To find salary levels for your field, visit salary.com or America's Career InfoNet (see Further Resources at the end of this section). These sites list salary ranges for jobs by region, generally calculated on forty hours a week. Use the annual rate to figure your hourly rate. For example, if you make $50,000 pretax per year working forty hours a week, fifty-two weeks a year, you are earning $961.54 each week ($50,000 ÷ 52 = $961.54). Divide that by forty hours a week, and you come up with $24 an hour. Then, if you're going to work twenty-five hours a week, multiply 25 × $24, which equals $600 a week, or $31,250 a year (52 weeks × $600 a week).

Ideally, you should be paid a similar rate for part-time work. If you're already working full-time for a company, and you're negotiating to recast your position as part-time, getting the same rate per hour shouldn't be a problem. Very few employers attempt to reduce salaries when employees opt to change to part-time.

You should also ask for prorated benefits. Remember, you usually need to ask for what you want. Part-time professionals should receive prorated health benefits, sick and vacation days, and retirement benefits and stock options. The U.S. Department of Labor's National Compensation Survey site (www.bls.gov/ncs) has benefits data, although the site is not particularly user-friendly. Associations in your field are also great sources for comparing compensation packages.

If you're seeking a part-time position from scratch—in other words, you don't have an "in" with the company but plan to enter as a new employee—it may be more of a challenge to get the same rate you would earn per hour as a full-timer. That's because many employers know that people are desperate for part-time work and are willing to compromise. Only you know what working part-time is worth to you. Sometimes it's worth less pay to get more quality time.

Still, there is a growing movement of impressive, aggressive people who are sick and tired of being paid less, who are demanding that they be paid what they're worth. Women especially need to work on this (visit the advocacy section of www.mothersandmore.org). The positions are out there, but you often have to fight for them, fight for your money and benefits, or create the position for yourself. To improve your negotiating skills, see Further Resources at the end of this section.

If you feel you have to compromise on the pay front to get a part-time position, don't despair—once you get into a company as a part-timer and prove your worth, you can negotiate for better pay. Many books, articles, and Web sites are devoted to the fine art of negotiating, and negotiating salaries in particular.

Everyone can use help in learning better negotiating skills, but women do seem to lag behind in this area. That's doubly unfortunate in this scenario because women still comprise the majority of part-timers. It's odd, too, given that women are generally very savvy about other money matters. Just think of all the time women put into researching home and life expenses and purchases. Why neglect this most important feature of life— the money you earn? Negotiating is a skill that can be learned— at the very least, you can improve your technique. Don't let fear stop you. The more you try it, the easier it becomes, and with practice, you will improve.

Note: Government organizations and other behemoth bureaucracies have set salary rates with little room for negotiation.

In general, hold off on any salary/benefits negotiations until the very end of the discussion. Wait until the offer or agreement is firmly in place. If you feel pressured, you can always say, "Could we hold off on the monetary discussion for a bit?" Know your lowest number, but start out mentioning a higher one. Try to get the other person to mention salary first and have some responses ready to go if you're not happy: "I was hoping for more because the median range for this position is . . ."

If a question or comment leaves you feeling like the proverbial deer in the headlights, don't be afraid to maneuver for more time with a comment such as, "Let me get back to you on that" or "Let me think about that, and I'll get back to you shortly."

FURTHER RESOURCES

- *Getting to Yes: Negotiating Agreement Without Giving In* by Roger Fisher, William L. Ury, and Bruce Patton
- AARP, www.aarp.org/money/careers
- America's Career InfoNet, www.acinet.org, sponsored by the U.S. Department of Labor, a great site for comparing salaries by job and region (from the main page, click on "Occupation Information" and follow the drop-down menu guidelines)
- *Be Heard the First Time: The Woman's Guide to Powerful Speaking* by Susan Miller; tips to improve business meeting and presentation skills and the voice itself
- National Compensation Survey, U.S. Department of Labor (www.bls.gov/ncs); surveys and data on earnings and benefits (good information but a difficult site to negotiate)
- Dr. Phil McGraw, www.drphil.com; follow links "Advice," "Money," "Career," or search for the article on "Surprising Facts about Women and Negotiating"
- Career-related site, www.Monster.com; see "Salary Center"
- www.rileyguide.com; see "Evaluating and Negotiating Job Offers" and salary data
- www.salary.com; for salary information and "Job Salary Negotiations & Tips"
- The Small Business Administration, www.sba.gov; search using the term "negotiating"
- The U.S. Equal Employment Opportunity Commission,

www.eeoc.gov/epa; see information on Equal Pay and Compensation Discrimination. According to this site, "The Equal Pay Act requires that men and women be given equal pay for equal work in the same establishment. The jobs need not be identical, but they must be substantially equal." If you feel you may be discriminated against, this is the place to begin your search.

- World at Work. The Professional Association for Compensation, Benefits and Total Rewards, www.worldatwork.org

General Negotiating Tips for Meetings

After you've done all your homework and written a fantastic proposal, submit the proposal in advance so your manager has a chance to read and digest the material. Arrange a time to discuss it.

- Practice your pitch with a friend or colleague; it will make a difference in delivery and results.
- Dress professionally to bolster your confidence.
- Listen carefully to the other person and be sensitive to his or her needs. Remember, that person wants to know what's in it for him or her. But use "I" phrases like "I need" and "I must" to bolster your point of view during the discussion.
- Agree on easier points first; come back to difficult issues at a later time.
- Present a range of options. For example, "I can work twenty to thirty hours a week."
- Speak in neutral tones; don't become too emotionally charged and don't be too negative.
- If you are uncertain about anything in the negotiating session, tell your employer you will think about it. *Never* make a final decision on the spot.
- Try to be appreciative and say thank you when you feel satisfied about the points discussed; it helps move the discussion along;

- Maintain your professionalism and try not to personalize the situation.
- Try to view the situation in gray, not black or white, terms.
- Ask whether your employer needs any additional information to help him or her understand the proposal or to help in making a decision.
- Exit gracefully.

REAL-LIFE EXAMPLE: VICE PRESIDENT OF MARKETING

A client of mine was at a company for nine and a half years when she decided to leverage her experience to change to a part-time situation so she could spend more time with her child. She felt her job could be broken down into specific parts despite the fact that she ran her own division. She was also convinced that she could perform the job in twenty hours as well as someone else could in forty. That was her pitch.

As a first course of action, she called competitors to determine what she would be worth as a freelancer. Then she spoke with her present company. This was the toughest negotiation in her life. To prepare, she wrote a detailed job description stating what she thought she could and couldn't do as a working parent. For example, commuting four days a week was too much. Because she had done salary research, she realized her value and negotiated to receive a large portion of her past salary.

The company had more work than it could handle and, therefore, was greatly in need of her skills and experience. It recognized her as a one-of-a-kind, superior performer and realized it would be difficult to find someone else who could perform as efficiently as she could. The bottom line—the company agreed to her proposal.

After her contract expired, she switched to another company, where she negotiated full benefits for part-time work. Her arrangements succeeded because she is a true dynamo who believes in her abilities and has the record to prove it.

I asked her what the greatest challenges and benefits are in changing from full-time to part-time. The greatest benefit for her is that she can now live and breathe. As a full-time employee, she was working herself to death. Now work is more of a sideline; as a part-timer, when she leaves, she leaves. Her priorities are her children. The pendulum swung from work as her primary focus to her children as her primary focus.

However, she has worked hard to make this work/life balance happen. She manages by delegating well at work and being highly organized. She now has no time to chat at the water cooler and has to hold her ground against those who challenge her leaving early. She is able to do this because of her confidence in her value to the organization even though she is not there full-time. For the most part, her team is loyal and committed. A few find her a nuisance since she's not there all the time, and they challenge her on this occasionally. She feels the need to prove to them that she can still perform at a very high level.

She sometimes varies her schedule and works more hours to show that she's willing and committed. Instead of being rigid, she increases her hours when she sees that more hours are needed and will be appreciated. In actuality, her part-time schedule makes her a better troubleshooter because she is not so entrenched in details and has more perspective. She also feels she has improved her decision-making skills and is more efficient.

After much thought and many discussions, she also began to understand the importance of taking time for herself. Now she takes one afternoon a week, three hours, to spend entirely on herself. The benefit of having more time and space is that it relaxes her and enables her to gain a fresh perspective. When she began to give herself more time and space, she also began to give her partner and others more time and space, and her relationships improved.

CHAPTER 6

How to Find the Best Part-Time Position

As we discussed in chapter 5, the best part-time positions are usually the result of a person adapting a full-time position to a part-time one, arranging a telecommuting option, or finding someone to job share a position. Linda Marks, Flex Group director of New Ways to Work, www.nww.org, backs this up: "Most good part-time and job-sharing positions are not listed anywhere. You have to create them from what is available."

Other options for high-quality part-time work, detailed in chapter 4, include working independently as a freelance agent or consultant or starting a part-time business.

That said, however, not everyone has a position that can be converted to part-time, and many don't want to deal with the challenges and inconsistencies of being a freelancer or entrepreneur.

For other part-time opportunities, the job market can be broken down into two categories: the formal or published job market and the informal or unpublished job market. When I refer to "published market," I'm talking about the sites and publications that post active job openings and solicit responses from job seekers. Only about 25 percent of jobs are publicized, and these can be found on Internet sites, newspapers, job boards, industry papers, etc.

The vast majority of jobs are unpublished. Think of the world of employment opportunities as a giant iceberg—the top juts out of the water (those are the listed openings), but the vast majority, including the best positions, are beneath the surface. Make sure you devote at least fifteen to twenty hours a week to your job search. Initially, you may have to "settle" for a position that's not perfect for you. That's okay, as long as you don't stop looking for the job that best matches your values, priorities, interests, skills, personality style, and needs.

Remember, the major difference between a successful and an unsuccessful job seeker is attitude. Everyone finds the job search difficult. Most of us suffer disappointments, but successful job seekers persevere. They don't quit until they succeed and succeed they do.

Organize your job search: plan job search activities daily, set goals, keep detailed records, and maintain deadlines.

Most important, evaluate your game plan continually. If your strategy isn't working, look realistically at what you are doing. Remember, the job search is a process, not an outcome. Remain flexible.

Published Markets

These are the sites and publications that post and list active job openings and solicit responses from job seekers.

Internet Searches

Many people turn first to the Internet in a job search. It's true that search engines have made it relatively easy to search for jobs by category, geographic location, and even salary. The Internet is a good place to start to get ideas about what's out there. These sites cover various part-time, freelance, job share (though not many), temporary, and seasonal positions.

Don't limit yourself to job search sites, however. Also, visit local, state, and national government Web sites for job listings. Follow your heart and interests—go to your "favorite" bookmarked sites. Many organizations and companies list job opportunities on their Web sites (see Resources below for listings of companies and associations).

Make sure your electronic resumes and cover letters are attachment ready (can be sent, retrieved, and posted over the Internet), and that the organization you're sending it to is willing to open attachments. There are many good books out there on creating resumes (see chapter 10 for extensive resume information). Many of the job-related Web sites listed under Further Resources also contain information about writing resumes and cover letters. Unless you're applying to one type of job only, I recommend that you have several versions of your resume tailored to apply to various positions. Three sites that offer good information on how to prepare your resume files so that they may be emailed and posted easily are:

- Quintessential Careers, www.quintcareers.com
- The Riley Guide, www.rileyguide.com
- www.job-hunt.org

There are, however, pitfalls to searching for jobs on the Internet:

- It can be time-consuming to find what you want.
- It can lull you into a sense of complacency. Only 5 percent to 20 percent of your job search time should be spent on the Internet. Most jobs are secured through networking, so don't hide behind your computer.
- Even though the sites are becoming more secure, if you post your resume, you always run the risk of privacy and confidentiality breaches.
- A zillion other people are cruising these sites as well; the competition is fierce.
- Some of the listings are outdated.
- You're a faceless commodity. It's hard to sell yourself by resume and cover letter alone.
- See www.job-hunt.org for the "Dirty Dozen Online Job Search Mistakes"

Despite these potential pitfalls, I know you're going to do a fair amount of Web surfing. In that case, here are some of the top sites, listed in alphabetical order, to get you started. In addition to job listings, many of these sites have career-related resources, such as tips on writing and preparing resumes and cover letters; a few also have salary information and discussion forums.

Remember, most of these sites have links that lead to links that lead to links. You could spend hours and hours jumping from site to site. After you've sent many a resume off into cyberspace, you could still be without the position you want. The Internet is a fantastic tool, but don't get too dependent on it, especially while searching for a part-time position. The best jobs come from networking, referrals, and other insider sources (see Networking in this chapter).

Note: The following list is only a sampling. Many of these sites come and go, but these were all current at publication.

ONLINE JOB SEARCH RESOURCES

- www.6figurejobs.com
- www.ajb.org; this is the job bank component of Career One Stop, sponsored by the U.S. Department of Labor. It has three sections: America's Career Infonet, careerinfonet.org, provides salary data, etc.; America's Job Bank, ajb.org, the "nation's largest online labor exchange"; and America's Service Locator, ServiceLocator.org, which includes information on job training, education, and unemployment benefits.
- www.academiccareers.com
- www.bestjobsusa.com
- www.careerbuilder.com; has a special link to part-time positions broken down into career categories.
- www.careers-in-business.com; specializes in jobs in business, finance, marketing, etc.
- www.careerjournal.com; the *Wall Street Journal*'s "executive career suite"
- www.careerresources.net; includes links to company Web sites
- www.careers.org; has multiple links to jobs by region and profession

- www.computerjobs.com; searchable by region
- www.coolworks.com
- www.craigslist.com; many people swear by this site, especially those seeking freelance and part-time positions
- www.dice.com, technology specialists
- http://dod.jobsearch.org; a resource for "military personnel transitioning to civilian work"
- www.eco.org; environmental careers
- www.eresumes.com
- www.escapeartist.com; information on jobs around the world
- www.execu-search.com; professional recruitment and temporary staffing
- www.freelanceworkexchange.com
- www.gadball.com; bills itself as a "free resume distribution site"
- www.guru.com; a "marketplace for freelance talent"
- www.hotjobs.com; Yahoo's job search site.
- http://jb-ge.hrdc-drhc.gc.ca; Canada's main job search site
- http://jobs.aol.com; AOL's job site (you can also access this site from the main AOL page)
- www.jobs.employmentguide.com
- www.job-hunt.org; many resources, including searches by state, creating "Cyber Safe" resumes, and "Choosing a Job Site"
- www.jobsearching.org, Professionals in Transition
- www.jobstar.org
- www.journalismjobs.com
- www.inkwelleditorial.com; all types of jobs in the publishing industry
- www.looking2hire.com; includes what the site refers to as "neighborhood" jobs
- www.monster.com
- www.monstertrak.com; a division of monster.com specifically for college students and recent graduates
- www.net-temps.com
- www.parttimejobstore.com; includes part-time salary surveys
- www.quintcareers.com; includes job bank, "salary wizard," and other resources.

- www.rileyguide.com; many resources, including salary guide and search by location
- www.sciencecareers.org
- www.snagajob.com
- www.TopUSAJobs.com
- www.usajobs.opm.gov; federal government jobs
- www.vjb.com; click on "careers" for a long list of related job posting sites
- www.worktree.com

COMPANY RESOURCES

See the Unsolicited Contact section in this chapter for a list of Web resources for finding particular companies and contacts, including "Best Places to Work" lists.

HOME-BASED BUSINESS RESOURCES

Many sites professing to cater to home-based businesses proliferate on the Web. Job search sites also feature categories for "home-based" business opportunities. Some are legitimate, but many are scams. See the detailed information on home-based businesses in chapter 4. Some legitimate outsourcing agencies are listed in this chapter under "Employment Agencies."

NEWSPAPERS AND TRADE ASSOCIATION PUBLICATIONS

Most of us are well acquainted with the "Help Wanted" sections of newspapers and trade association magazines, but make sure you're not limiting yourself to the print editions. Go to the publications' Web sites for the most up-to-date listings. To find links to a newspaper of interest, go to newspapers.com.

Association Web sites are good places to look for specific subject-related positions. In fact, many associations have limited their printed materials because of high publication and mailing costs; the vast majority post most of their news and job openings on their Web sites. You can find the following directories at your library: *The Encyclopedia of Associations* and *Weddle's Guide to Association Websites: For Recruiters and Job Seekers*; the latter includes more than 2,500 Web sites. Both books organize associations by career field and geographic location.

Also, search the following sites for links to associations:

- American Society for Association Executives, www.asae net.org
- The Internet Public Library, www.lpl.org; search directories

NONPROFIT JOB SITES

- The Foundation Center, http://fdncenter.org; has a "job corner" link
- www.guidestar.org; has a job link under "classifieds"
- www.idealist.org; lists jobs, volunteer opportunities, and internships

SPECIAL AUDIENCE SITES

These sites feature job bank lists and career resources for women and minorities:

- www.advancingwomen.com
- www.disabilityinfo.gov
- www.imdiversity.com; provides career and self-development information for all minorities
- www.saludos.com; Hispanic
- www.women.com; links to a wide range of associations, job fairs, etc.

Unpublished Markets

Many openings are not posted. These positions may circulate privately through informal or formal networking systems, or an employer may only consider hiring for a new position or replacing an employee and is seeking the right motivation, opportunity, or person to spark the employer into action.

Employment Agencies

The opportunities for part-time positions through traditional employment and headhunter agencies are sparse. I recommend that you do not place too much hope and emphasis on them. However, outsourcing agencies hire people to work out of their homes to field telephone calls, mainly in sales and customer service. Here are some sites to contact for more information:

- www.Alpineaccess.com
- www.callcenteroptions.com
- www.gowillow.com
- www.intellicare.com
- www.vipdesk.com
- www.virtualassistants.com
- www.workathomeagent.com
- www.workingsolutions.com

Networking

Many top-notch part-time, reduced-schedule, and flexible jobs can be found through networking. For example, I know someone who got a good part-time position by casually mentioning to a fellow volunteer at an ocean conservation organization that she would like to work part-time. It so happened that her fellow volunteer was also on the Board of Directors of an organization that was looking for a qualified part-time professional to fill an as yet unadvertised position. She got the interview and the job. Sound like a lucky coincidence? Perhaps. The point is, she never would have known about the position if she hadn't been out in the world talking to and connecting with others—and telling people that she was looking for a particular job!

In addition, a client of mine needed to work part-time as a lawyer while he pursued his creative interests. He contacted a few of his former clients, and they directed him to a firm that needed a part-time attorney. If he had not reached out, he never would have secured the position.

The "hidden" job market is an important source of jobs. Start by networking with those who share your interests. What groups do you belong to: a religious congregation, a civic organization, a professional group, or a university alumni network? Do you belong to any groups, including Web forums, that relate to your hobbies or political affiliations? Always look to your own base when networking. Remember that friends and relatives are also part of your networking world. Talk up your needs wherever possible and appropriate. Everyone you know may know someone who can lead you to a potential opportunity.

Networking Opportunities

ASSOCIATIONS AND OTHER PROFESSIONAL ORGANIZATIONS AND INSTITUTIONS

You definitely want to network with those who share your business and professional interests. Most fields have formal organizations that cover practically every field—from the Flying Funeral Directors of America to the Sponge and Chamois Institute. Many have Web sites and/or newsletters and magazines that list job openings, contacts, and news-related items that may lead to current and future job openings.

They also have conferences, meetings, seminars, and workshops, which offer the best opportunities for making face-to-face contact with people who can connect you not only with potential opportunities, but also with key decision makers in your field.

Even if a position isn't open at the time, if you tell someone you're looking and you give that person a card and an occasional gentle email reminder, your name will be on the top of the list when opportunity arises. Remember, people quit jobs, people are fired from jobs, people get promoted—all of which leave openings. If you've already laid a foundation, you're in a good position to be considered. In fact, you may not even be looking for a job, but one of your colleagues may contact you to gauge your level of interest in a possible opening because he or she remembers meeting you at a conference.

Associations and organizations aren't limited to your field of interest. There are also associations, organizations, and clubs that unite people along shared hobbies and interests or by gender, nationality, region, and age. See the Special Audience Sites listed in this chapter.

ALUMNI ORGANIZATIONS

Don't forget your alma maters—whether grade school, high school, college, or graduate school. Many people are extremely devoted to their former schools, and quite a few are sentimental about classmates. Start by searching for your schools on the Internet; universities are obviously the best place to start as they have Web sites, career planning and placement offices, and alumni network systems. Don't forget to search the faculty department as well; former teachers are usually flattered to be contacted for suggestions regarding your career direction. Even if they're not flattered, they may point out good leads and resources.

Internet sites will help you find your fellow alumni. Check out:

- www.alumni.net
- www.classmates.com

Listservs, Newsgroups, Message Boards, and Chat Rooms

Listservs are discussion or emailing lists maintained either by formal organizations or by loosely formed groups of people who share an interest, line of work, or hobby. Although even an informal group requires at least one diligent person to run the listserv, most are free. Really, it's just a fancy name for a group email list, whereby people can send out questions, post announcements, etc. Topics go out to everyone on the list, and you usually can reply either to the group as a whole or to individual members.

This is a great way to get a lot of insider information. We all live hectic lives far apart from one another. Listservs unite us and put us back into the gossip/info loop.

Some listservs are subscription–based, others are invitation only. The best way to find a listserv in your area of interest is to ask your friends, colleagues, and peers or a related professional association if they can refer you to a listserv. Then all you need to do to subscribe is send an email to the specific host. Coollist.com provides links for joining mailing lists and starting one.

Newsgroups and message boards are discussion groups on the Internet on which you can post a message on the equivalent of an electronic bulletin board, and others can reply to you. These are quite informal, and the fact that anyone can hide behind a veil of anonymity makes it a free-for-all exchange. Some people post their real names, others use aliases. Some newsgroups and message boards are monitored, so they have to be more civilized; for others—anything goes. The big search engines, Google, Yahoo, and AOL to name a few, list many newsgroups and message boards. Individual sites also have message boards and chat rooms. In the latter, conversation takes place in real time.

See the list of employment related sites in this chapter for job-related newsgroups, message boards, and chat rooms.

Career and Job Fairs

These are great places to get your resume into the hands of employers who are actively looking to hire. They're also a great way to meet and network with others in your field. Even if you're not planning on handing out a resume, you can see what's out there and get a sense of individual companies.

- Dress professionally even if you're "just looking."
- Carry your resumes and other related materials in a professional-looking portfolio or packet.
- If you know there are companies there in which you are interested, do some homework, so you can make some relevant comments or ask pertinent questions.

- Be sure you have pencils/pens, notebook, and business cards with you.
- Put on your best interview face—be professional, direct, courteous, and conscious of the potential employer's time. Don't hog the spotlight if there's a long line behind you.

Many of the Internet job sites listed at the beginning of this chapter have information on job fairs, what to ask, strategies, etc. The following sites list job fairs:

- www.americasjobfair.com
- www.careerfairs.com
- www.nationaljobfairs.com
- www.womenforhire.com

Volunteer

Volunteering is another great way to carve out a part-time position for yourself. If you are very careful and thorough and find a volunteer assignment that matches well with your skills and interests, you can find out what the organization needs and propose a part-time job.

I recently met a woman who said her experience has been to go from volunteer to part-time work. Volunteering is clearly a way to develop skills and relationships that enable you to get a part-time position.

Many local and state government Web sites list volunteer opportunities. Also think about organizations that you have a passion for and interest in and approach them directly. Most nonprofit organizations are looking for volunteers.

FURTHER RESOURCES
Various Internet sites match volunteers with specific needs. You select your areas of interest, and the program provides a list of relevant opportunities. You can also search for volunteer positions by location—local, national, or international.

- www.Idealist.org
- www.NetworkForGood.com
- www.SERVEnet.org
- www.USAFreedomCorps.gov
- www.VolunteerMatch.org
- www.volunteer-referral.com

Tips for Effective Networking

- Speak to as many people as you can. Don't be afraid to tell people you're looking for a certain type of job; ask them to think of you if they hear anything. Two or three brief follow-ups are a good idea, but don't pressure people.
- Be clear: identify your objective, skill set, target market, and time frame. If the only information you circulate is that you need a job, you're unlikely to be effective. As much as possible, be specific when telling people what kind of job you're looking for and with what type of organization. Without this information, it is difficult for people to help you, even if they want to. Whether or not people want to support you or even pass the word about you depends partly on whether they believe you are qualified. Why should people risk their own reputation by suggesting you for a position for which you're not qualified? Use examples of what you've done.
- Be authentic, open, honest, and positive about your job search intentions. No one likes to feel manipulated. At the same time, most people understand and appreciate the necessity of networking. People generally like to help someone else; one day they may need the same favor.
- Create a list of "select" organizations for which you would like to work and gather information. The more you know about the organizations, the better able you are to determine which ones are most likely to be a good fit for you and which are more likely to have an upcoming need. Make sure you know the names of the key people in the organization.

- Seek advice: many people love to help and offer ideas and suggestions. Their advice may result in likely organizations you had not considered. It may also lead to additional contacts inside companies and organizations.
- Referral generation. One of the main goals of networking is getting referrals. One person refers another to you who the first person believes can be helpful. A client of mine once coined the phrase, "work your net," I thought it was descriptive. A person is more likely to meet with you via an introduction or referral.
- When you do get a lead from someone in your network, it's best to prepare for the initial phone call with a script. For example: "I am Lynn Berger, and I'm looking for a part-time counseling position. Debra Laks suggested I contact you. Debra and I know one another from a professional association. Do you have any ideas or information that might lead me to potential opportunities? Furthermore, do you have time on Friday afternoon to meet for a cup of coffee?" As you can see, I did not ask for a job––only an introduction.
- Returning the favors: one key to networking is to remember what you can give. Look for opportunities to assist someone else. Listen carefully for clues, including the person's interests and hobbies. This helps to build relationships. Give and you shall receive.
- Send a note of thanks. You may send an email or, believe it or not, many people appreciate a simple handwritten note.

Potential Networking Mistakes

When networking during a job search, people make a number of common errors. One is inquiring only about currently available jobs. The chief problem with this approach is that most people may not be aware of current available positions, nor will they be able to assess which one(s) may be suitable for you. In addition, the person may then become frustrated by his or her inability to help. This can lead to a dead end because there is nothing worthwhile to discuss.

Proper networking etiquette includes asking:

- if the person has any ideas/suggestions for you, and
- if the person knows of anyone to contact in your area(s) of interest.

The second frequent misjudgment inexperienced job seekers make is that they sometimes try to network without a mutual interest. People who have a common bond are more likely to be interested in helping you. For people who do not know you, this will be more difficult. In job search networking, there always needs to be some sort of common interest.

FURTHER RESOURCES

- *Million Dollar Networking: The Sure Way to Find, Keep and Grow Your Business* by Andrea Nierenberg (Capital, 2005)
- *Nonstop Networking: How to Improve Your Life, Luck, and Career* by Andrea Nierenberg (Capital, 2002)

Unsolicited Contact: "Cold Calling" via Letter or Email

This type of search starts with research. Make a list of all the organizations in which you're interested and visit their Web sites to see if there are any openings. If they don't list a position that interests you, familiarize yourself with the company from its Web site, annual reports, newsletters, and magazines. Then send the company a cover letter and resume pitching for a particular position. Contact specific people directly. Research the names and titles of key personnel by area of interest. For example, contact the vice president of training and development, director of employment, etc. Make sure you have the right name and spelling for the contact.

When following this approach, be courteous and professional. Do not cold call with casual emails or phone calls. A formal introductory letter or email is much better. You also must know when to hold 'em and know when to fold 'em. In other words, don't pester people to the point of annoyance. Learn to take a hint so you don't lose a valuable contact.

Remember that this approach is a percentage game. The majority of letters will go in the trash can, but some will make it into a real file and some will elicit a return. People appreciate initiative—and if you plan your pitch letters and personalize them for the organization, you can tap into some great, unheralded opportunities.

The following sites have information on finding the Web sites for particular companies or corporations, so you can contact the corporation or business directly and search its site for job openings and research benefits, etc. These sites provide links to companies for free; some charge for more comprehensive reports:

- AARP, www.aarp.org; lists "best employers for workers over 50"
- www.bestjobsusa.com; includes company profiles and best places to work
- www.business.com
- Chambers of Commerce, www.chambers.com
- www.companiesonline.com
- www.corporateinformation.com; links to company Web sites and provides free "sample" profiles and comprehensive profiles for a fee
- Dunn and Bradstreet's Million Dollar Database, www.dnb mdd.com/mddi
- www.forbes.com/lists; best places to work list
- www.fortune.com; best companies to work for list
- www.greatplacetowork.com; "Best of" lists
- www.hoovers.com
- www.standardandpoors.com
- www.thomasregister.com
- www.workingmother.com; has a "best companies" for parents

- www.yahoo.com; click on "business" under web directory listings, then follow the links to find the Web sites for your companies of interest

Companies that Offer Benefits to Part-Time Staff

Here's a *sampling*—and I stress the word "sampling"—of companies that offer partial benefits to part-time employees. I just want to demonstrate that if you need benefits and want to work part-time, you can find companies that fit the bill. But you'll have to do some research.

AARP, www.aarp.org/money/careers, has a "featured employer" listing that includes information on the type of benefits included. Also search the listed company resources in this section.

- Borders
- Container Store
- Foxwoods Resort Casino
- Home Depot
- Publix Supermarkets
- Starbucks
- UPS
- Wegmans
- Government jobs and universities are also good places to look for jobs that also provide benefits

(These companies were included in "Nothing Partial About These Benefits" by Elayne Robertson Demby, an article on the Society for Human Resource Management Web site, www.shrm.org.)

Know Your Transferable Skills

Employers often look for the following skills in part-time employees—people who are well organized, service-oriented, proficient in computer skills, resourceful, and independent. These are clearly transferable skills.

WHAT ARE TRANSFERABLE SKILLS?

Transferable skills are skills that can be applied in a wide variety of work settings to a wide variety of tasks. It is good to emphasize them in cover letters, job applications, and interviews. They include:

- Communication skills: Writes in clear concise language, speaks to individuals and groups proficiently, listens well, and expresses ideas clearly.
- Interpersonal skills: Works well with colleagues, subordinates, and bosses.
- Interviewing skills: Elicits necessary information from people, generates trust.
- Supervisory skills: Takes control of work of others, directs work of others.
- Public Relations skills: Serves as representative to others, writes press releases.
- Sales skills: Work well with customers, anticipates needs readily.
- Negotiating skills: Resolves differences between parties in difficult situations.
- Teaching/instructing skills: Trains others as appropriate.
- Leadership skills: Takes charge, motivates others, makes decisions.
- Public speaking skills: Talks publicly, prepares remarks, good presentation skills.
- Problem-solving skills: Evaluates alternatives to a problem, analyzes situations and solutions well.
- Budget management skills: Keeps control of budgets, manages and dispenses funds.
- Organizing/managing/coordinating skills: Takes charge of events, manages people.
- Research skills: Assesses a situation, identifies the resources necessary for solutions.

- Planning and development skills: Senses an idea and works toward implement it.

TRANSFERABLE SKILLS EXERCISE

Go through the list of transferable skills and match concrete examples of your accomplishments and experiences with a given skill. Don't limit your experience to paid positions; think about skills you've used at home, in organizations, or in volunteer positions, for example, organizing skills—planned, organized, and implemented the Girl Scout cookie drive. Be sure to include any earnings.

Another example is involvement in planning any unique personal and professional events. You may have initiated, planned, and executed a charity event. This experience and the skills you used can be transferred to an event planning/conference meeting position. Also think about internships you have had. Those experiences are valid, and the skills you gained from them can be easily transferred to another position.

If You Don't Have the Skills for the Job You Want, Go Back to School

If you're interested in making a career and lifestyle change, you may need to go back to school. Don't let this stop you. Nursing and teaching, for example, are much-sought skills in today's part-time market. Investigate how much schooling you'd need to switch careers. Many teaching certificate programs now offer streamlined certification for those with professional skills who would like to switch careers to teaching.

Check out the colleges and universities in your area and consider online study. Distance learning, as it's sometimes called, can be a viable way to expand your skill set. Taking classes online can easily fit your lifestyle. I know people who have participated in online learning, from taking an online writing class to getting a doctoral degree.

If you choose to get an online degree or certification, don't forget that you still need to get out and meet people in the field. Don't use online learning as an excuse to hide behind your computer. Many universities and colleges now have online learning programs. If you enroll in a school that's within a reasonable distance, you can have the best of both worlds—the ease of online study at home and a real place to network face-to-face with others.

RESOURCES

- www.edsurf.net; connects to the University of Phoenix Online
- www.geteducated.com
- www.onlinelearning.net; for teachers
- www.seminarinformation.com
- www.tregistry.com; training seminars and workshops
- United States Distance Learning Association, www.usdla.org

Hot Part-Time Careers

You can always increase your chances of finding a job that fits your schedule, salary, and benefit needs and, perhaps, all three, if you focus on those markets with a big demand for employees.

- Accounting/finance/compliance: These are growing fields due to increased government regulation (e.g., the Sarbanes-Oxley Act). These fields offer professional positions where you stand a good chance of negotiating the big three: salary, benefits, and flexibility.
- Child care: High demand, but the money still isn't good. Decent potential for flexibility in terms of hours, but not place, for example, you can't telecommute child care. Medium potential for benefits, low potential for salary.
- Computer support: Always in demand for offices and home businesses. High potential for negotiating salary, benefits, and flexibility.
- Elder care: High demand due to longer life spans and off-

spring who are unwilling or unable to take on the care. Flexibility and benefit options are good if working for an organization. They're generally not good for those working as independent caretakers. Still a low-paying career, but aging baby boomers may change that by providing opportunities for creative entrepreneurs who come up with more stimulating, thoughtful care and activities for an aging population.

- Health care (see the following section for more details)
- Mortgage consulting: Salary, benefits, and flexibility options are good.
- Pet services: Growing demand and good flexibility; salary and benefits are still low.
- Professional home inspector: Not as much flexibility because you have to respond to clients, but you don't necessarily have to work long hours; good salary if independent but no benefits.
- Real estate broker: Often requires a lot of time and effort to be truly successful; potential for good salary but no benefits.
- Teachers: online, in the classroom, and as tutors. Flexibility and potential for benefits are good, but salary is still low, especially for adjuncts and substitutes. There's more money potential in tutoring, but no benefits if working independently and need to be available for clients.
- Virtual assistants (due to the growth in home-based business): Flexibility, good salary if independent but no benefits.
- Web designers. Flexibility and salary are good. Benefits potential good if you work for a company.

One of the Hottest in Terms of Demand and Creative Benefits

HEALTH CARE/NURSING

The demand for nurses is increasing. The health care industry is expected to require "one million new and replacement nurses by 2010," according to the Bureau of Labor Statistics (BLS).

Currently, an estimated 125,000 nursing positions are available.

As a result of labor shortages, hospitals and other employers go out of their way to keep employees happy. Though salaries are still arguably low, a recent lengthy advertisement in the *New York Times Magazine* cites BLS statistics that place median earnings for nurses in 2002 at $49,840. That's approximately $3,800 more than the median for teachers and almost $11,000 more than the pay for social workers.

The benefits and flexibility options for nurses are increasingly good and creative. For example, employers offer flexible shifts, part-time positions, and self-scheduling, and some offer on-site or nearby child care centers. Signing bonuses and double time and a half for holidays are not unusual. Part-time nurses are usually eligible for health benefits, and some employers now offer matching 401(k) benefits, a highly desired and hard-to-get benefit for part-timers.

Some hospitals even offer what they call "out of the box" benefits. In an advertisement for health care jobs, one company in the Washington, D.C., metropolitan area mentioned benefits for wellness programs, tuition reimbursement, short-term disability and long-term care insurance coverage, and matching 401(k) funds.

The field is also very flexible. You can work in a hospital setting, as a home care assistant, in a doctor's office, or as a traveling nurse. Home care situations often afford you the opportunity to make your own schedule, which, in turn, lets you juggle work and family responsibilities. Working in a doctor's office has the advantage of little or no work on the weekends, and in some situations, you can leave to be home for the children when they arrive home from school. A very interesting and exciting opportunity is working as a traveling nurse. You can travel anywhere from Alaska, to Mexico, to Hawaii for thirteen weeks at a time. Housing and benefits are paid for. The downside for many is that it's a transient lifestyle; however, for the adventurous, this could be just what the doctor ordered.

Because the demand for nurses is high, enrollment in nursing programs is rising—by 10.6 percent in 2004 alone, the fourth consecutive year of such increases, according to the American Association of Colleges of Nursing. That may cool off demand eventually, but with the baby boomer generation turning the corner, demand should remain relatively high, especially in elder care.

More and more men are turning to nursing as a career, and others are choosing nursing as a second, midlife career.

REAL-LIFE EXAMPLE: NURSE

I interviewed a part-time nurse at a major Northeast hospital who currently works on a casual or "self-scheduling" basis. She is valued enough that she can tell her employer when she's available. She loves what she does and finds her job very rewarding; she is gratified to know that she has made a difference in someone's life. She also finds the environment very supportive, with management willing to make allowances for maternity leave, family illnesses, etc.

One challenge of being a part-time nurse is trying to keep your skills up to par when you work infrequently. There are many continuing education requirements and mandatory training. Another challenge is that the work is exhausting and includes no downtime. She also said the paperwork is endless; every time she goes in to work, there are new forms and new guidelines.

Still, she finds nursing a family-friendly career, both personally rewarding and flexible.

CHAPTER 7

Perfect for Parents and Other Caregivers

Now that I have a baby, my original intention of returning to my former position no longer feels right. This is causing me a great deal of anxiety and confusion because I've spent my entire life, up to this point, preparing for my career. I want to be more in control of my professional activities, but still have time to be with my child. I don't think my previous work demands will fit into my new life. My values have shifted; yet I'm not prepared to completely abandon working.

Does this scenario sound familiar? There is nothing new about the conflicts and pressures parents feel. Since parenthood is one of life's milestones, it often makes us question our careers and try to find the appropriate balance between professional and personal needs. Is it really possible to pursue a professional life while raising a family?

The answer is yes, of course it is. For those who want to spend more time with their families yet need to work and for those who can afford to be stay-at-home parents yet need the intellectual stimulation that work provides, part-time could be the perfect option.

Parents aren't the only ones who need greater flexibility to take care of family members. Let's not forget that more and more people face the prospect of caring for aging parents. Longer life spans may be a blessing of modern technology and improved nutrition, but greater longevity also means a greater possibility of chronic disease. Still others need to take care of ailing siblings or other loved ones.

As I've already discussed, many types of flexible opportunities are available, from starting a home business to negotiating a part-time position with your company. There's also job sharing and seasonal work. If you can't cut your time in half, you can still reduce it or make your work life more flexible. All that limits you right now is your imagination. Even finances can be worked out with creativity (see chapter 2).

How to Make Part-Time Work for You as a Parent

The stress of working forty hours a week or more is well documented. With a part-time schedule, you'll have more time to savor moments with your family; to take care of yourself physically and emotionally; and to schedule doctor, dentist, and school appointments.

It's a chance to get the best of both worlds—the stimulation and self-esteem associated with external accomplishments and the peace-of-mind and self-esteem associated with having a more manageable personal life.

You may find that you or your partner only want to work reduced hours in the early childhood years, then go back to work full-time when your children are school age. An increasing number of parents, however, are finding that they need to be home after school during the teenage years.

Whenever you choose to do it, the first thing you need to do is work out a budget (see chapter 2). You need to figure out how much it's costing you to work. For example, how much are you paying in day care? In commuting costs? On wardrobe and dry cleaning? On lunches and take-out? Unless, you're in a very high-paying career, the likelihood is that you're probably not making that much net profit. With some ingenuity, you could make that same "net profit" in part-time work, especially if you work at home or during school hours.

Though average child care costs vary for a number of reasons, the cost for most people is substantial. Consider these figures:

- "Today, average child-care costs are roughly $4,000 per child per year—and substantially higher for families in metropolitan areas" (The Annie E. Casey Foundation, www.aecf.org).

- The average child care costs in urban areas for full-time care of an infant was more than "$6,032 per year for child care centers, and more than $5,000 per year for family child care" (2006, The Legal Momentum, Family Initiative, www.legalmomentum.org).

- In *The Unofficial Guide to Childcare*, Ann Douglas reports that average day care costs run about $420 per month, while private nannies can charge up to $2,000 or more per month.

According to MsMoney.com, "By the time extra work expenses are subtracted from a second salary of $24,000 a year, the take-home pay is approximately $219 a month, or a whopping $2,628 per year." When you start thinking about your financial situation in this light, you can begin to see that a reduced schedule might not hurt your pocketbook as much as you think. And the intangibles you gain—extra time for yourself and your children, better health, and less stress—more than make up for the scarifies.

As you think about what part-time career path might be the best for you, match your work options with your present values and priorities (see chapter 3). That way any reduction in salary and benefits will be made up in better health, greater satisfaction, and general well-being.

Keeping Skills Up to Date and Reentering the Job Market

Another important benefit of working part-time during the intensive parenting years is that you'll keep your skill level up and your resume current. For those who opt out of the work world altogether, they may find reentry intimidating and more challenging. If you keep your computer skills current, your contacts and networks fresh, and you have some recent accomplishments or projects to put on your resume, you'll be in a much better position to step up your career later, if you decide to do that.

Certain fields such as health, law, accounting, and technology change rapidly. Working part-time allows you to keep pace with new developments and training. Working part-time is also a way to keep your foot in the door should you decide later to go full-time.

If you're already well established in your career, and you are a middle-aged person who needs to take care of elderly parents, working part-time offers not only extra income, but the opportunity to get much needed social interaction and validation as well.

FURTHER RESOURCE

- *Now What Do I Do? The Woman's Guide to a New Career* by Jan Cannon, Ph.D.

REAL-LIFE EXAMPLES:

Remember, you're not alone. Plenty of others have faced the challenges of blending work and family life:

- Amy wanted and needed to keep her position in the corporate world, but working five days a week was overwhelming to her. I suggested that she ask her employer if she could work four days. She resisted because she thought her employer would never allow her to restructure her work schedule. But after our conversation, she began to realize that the company's cost of hiring and training a new employee, as well as her contribution to the firm four-fifths of the time, was significant. She presented her situation in a very convincing manner, and her employer agreed to her request.

- Susan, a registered nurse, is very interested in the field of holistic nursing. She also wanted to be home with her son as much as possible. She decided to return to school part-time to establish additional credentials in holistic nursing. She now works part-time in her new field of interest and has more control over her work schedule than she had before.

- Ben realized, after spending time at home, that there was a need for additional child safety products. He also had a talent for inventing and great interest in that area. He is now exploring the possibility of patenting a new child safety product and looking for a new job. He hopes his new venture will succeed, and he will not need to work in a more traditional job.

- Caryl raised three children and went back to school for a degree in library science, when her children were past school age. Her first job was as a part-time librarian. She liked the job very much and began to work more hours. Over time she took on more responsibilities, and ten years later, she became the director of the library.

Instead of seeing your situation as a dilemma—parenting versus career as a negative—view it as a way to make a very positive, meaningful change in your life. Breaking free from old value systems may seem difficult at first; however, the best news is that this stage in your life has the potential to be extremely fulfilling and satisfying.

TIP

Be diligent in your search for a position. Don't give in easily (see chapter 5). If you want benefits, look for a position with benefits. It may take a while to find the right fit—you've got to be determined. Take a lesser job if you have to and keep looking for the right one.

Spouse/Partner Agreement

I always recommend to my clients that they discuss changing their work situation with their spouse or significant other. Again, this may seem obvious, but many people try to make the decision without sufficient input from their partner.

You need to address your partner's concerns as well as your own. Usually one person is more comfortable than the other with the decision. The best way to come to a mutual decision is through communication and discussing each other's opinions, concerns, and ideas.

Making a decision like this usually prompts you to come to an understanding about your lifestyle needs and family goals. For example, one partner may be stressed out about the financial sacrifice if the other wants to change to less than full-time work. That partner might feel the additional burden of being the primary breadwinner. Determining a household budget with which you both feel comfortable is vital.

Be open about the shift in priorities that may be necessary as you make financial adjustments. Questions may come up such as: How important are materialistic goals? What specific sacrifices will we have to make?

You also need to be aware of how roles within the home might change. It's helpful to discuss the breakdown of household chores, for instance. You and your partner must understand the lifestyle needs and goals that come up at this time to move ahead in a fruitful and fulfilling way.

Last but not least, put your agreement in writing, but don't be afraid to alter and update as necessary.

The Web site, workoptions.com, offers a free "spousal support checklist for talking about going part-time."

Good News about Multiple Roles and Stress

Whether you're reducing your professional workload from full-time to part-time or going back to work part-time after staying at home as a parent, you might find the competing demands stressful initially. I recommend taking it slow. And take heart—there's significant good news about multiple roles and stress. Several studies have examined the relationship between the number of roles a person has and the positive effect of those roles on energy levels. Yes, you read correctly, a *positive* effect. The theory, known as "expansion hypothesis," is presented in *Social Roles, Gender and Psychological Distress.* The authors argue that the rewards women receive in terms of self-esteem, recognition, prestige, and financial remuneration more than offset the cost of adding on new roles.

Other research further supports the positive association between the number of roles a woman occupies and her psychological well-being. Women in the study who had multiple life roles (mother, wife, employee) were less depressed and had higher self-esteem than did women and men who had fewer life roles.

Personally, I can confirm the multiple roles and stress theory. When I feel overwhelmed in one area of my life, I gain perspective and buffer the stress by focusing on another area. This lessens the intensity of what may appear to be an all-consuming issue.

For example, whether I am experiencing stress in either my personal or work life, I find switching gears to the other refreshing and rejuvenating. For example, as a parent of a young child, I'm often faced with situations where a few minutes of reflection and objectivity can benefit the situation. When problems come up at work, for example, a computer breakdown, I try to focus on something else until it can be resolved.

Paid employment in particular has been found to have beneficial health effects for women when there is a match between a women's desire for employment and her work. The social support that work relationships provide also appears to improve health.

In fact, some women derive greater satisfaction from employment roles than from traditional roles as wife, mother, or community volunteer. Even though employed women have work-related stressors, they appear to be better off than women who are not employed.

So juggling part-time work and parenthood can actually help to reduce stress. Your relationship with your spouse or partner may improve as you develop a new sense of perspective and enjoy new experiences. People who work outside the home often find that they become more interesting to themselves and to others. Feelings of self-worth increase, and you achieve a sense of control and accomplishment, which, in turn, enables you to cope more easily with the pressures of daily life.

It is important to note that the more positive a person's experience is at work, the less likely that person is to experience role overload. In other words, it's the quality of the experiences within the roles that enhances your well-being. And that's what I'm trying to get you to examine in this book—finding the right mix of quality roles for the lifestyle you desire.

Good for Employers, Too

Though there's still need for improvement, companies are slowly realizing that if they want to hang on to quality employees, they need to be flexible, particularly where women are concerned. It's well documented that today's workers want more flexibility in dealing with their lives and careers. As you seek to negotiate a part-time position (see chapter 5), or as you go into the world in search of one, it's vital to know how family-friendly policies can improve the outlook for companies as well.

Claudia H. Deutsch reports in "Behind the Exodus of Executive Women: Boredom" that women outnumber men in managerial and professional positions," yet leave before they make it to the top, not because of the pressure but because they look around and ask, Is this all there is in life? Companies can ill afford this exodus of talent, so they are starting to adopt policies that help women (and men) balance their lives better. According to Deutsch, researchers at Catalyst, a nonprofit consulting business, show that "women have the same ambitions to get to the top as men.... But it is only in the last few years that companies have been acting on that knowledge." Other findings reported in the article include:

- Major companies have been training women in time management. "Procter [& Gamble] improved its retention by 25 percent over the last five years and has increased the number who moved from mid-level to senior jobs."

- Other companies have initiated "women's networks, coaching and mentoring programs, and family-balance policies."

One well-publicized success story is the Vista Rx program instituted by Pfizer. Kathleen Donovan, vice president for human resources at Pfizer, writes in a 2001 article that "the issue of staff retention" became a problem and that managers were "seeing a growing need to offer their sales professionals assistance with balancing the rigorous demands of a full-time sales rep with new or increasing demands of home and family."

Pfizer's solution was to create the Vista Rx program, which offers part-time work with full-time benefits to top performers who have an average of ten years' experience. In the program, sales representatives work 60 percent of the schedule of their full-time counterparts. Participants choose their own hours but still must meet challenging objectives, a combination that has enabled people to become very focused and efficient.

It turned out to be a "win-win proposition for both employer and employee." Needless to say the program is popular with employees. It's also proven its worth from a business perspective. According to Donovan, Vista Rx has become a "strategic tool," helping the company to meet a wide range of business challenges.

Working mothers comprised the bulk of the initial Vista Rx sales force, but some working fathers participated as well, as did those who simply wanted more time to enjoy life's pleasures.

Tips for Finding Family-Friendly Companies

I suggest that people explore family-friendly companies that offer on-site child care or other options. Do your research. You can start online and research Web sites, family-friendly company lists, and work/life balance Web sites. Talking to people about their companies is an excellent way to determine whether they are family friendly. Get a feel for the organization's corporate culture.

If you're on an interview, notice how people relate to one another. Subtle signs include pictures of family on desks and children's art projects on the walls. I recommend that you set up your interview for very early in the morning or later in the evening to see how many people are in the office at that time— a telling sign.

During the negotiation phase, you can inquire about benefits. Be creative and try to discover if there are any work/life balance programs. Get a sense of how they're used and if they're successful. You may be able to speak to other current employees regarding the company's support of working parents. It's most important to have your supervisor's support for work/life balance issues. One way to determine his or her level of support is to try to speak to the people who presently work for that supervisor. Many managers and supervisors recognize the benefits of helping employees see to their family needs.

Pat Katepoo, a work/life adviser who spearheads www. workoptions.com, has some good suggestions for identifying family-friendly companies:

- Contact your local chapter of the Society of Human Resources Management (SHRM); on shrm.org, click on "community" for chapter listings. Local human resources (HR) managers are likely to know top family-friendly employers in your area.

- Several cities now publish their own regional listings of family-friendly employers, nominated and selected by the community. Call your local chamber of commerce to find out if your city publishes such a list.

FURTHER RESOURCE

- See *Working Mothers* magazine's famous annual "100 Best Companies for Working Mothers," www.workingmother.com. For links to other "best companies to work for" lists, see chapter 6.

Part-Time Work Is Good for Your Kids, Too

It's seems obvious that having a loving parent oversee a child a significant portion of the child's waking day is a positive thing. But the flip side is that it's also good for children to see their parents working and happy.

According to a study, titled "Ask the Children," by Ellen Galinsky of the Families and Work Institute, being a working parent does not have undue influence on a "child's health, development, school readiness, and success." Other factors are significant when it comes to predicting how children assess their parents' parenting skills, but whether their mothers work is not one of them.

Ellen Galinsky hopes the results of the study will end the old debate about whether mothers should work. Another debate that she'd like to change is the one that deals with quality time versus quantity time. Time is not on the top of children's lists either. Only 10 percent wish for more time with their mothers and 15.5 percent for more time with their fathers. Mainly, the children wish their parents would be less stressed and less tired: 34 percent make this wish for their mothers and 27.5 percent for fathers. Interestingly, only 2 percent of parents guess that their children wish to reduce their parental stress and fatigue.

Time is still important—the more time children report spending with their parents, the more positively they feel they are being parented. However, the more significant point is that children want parents who are calm and relatively stress free. They don't like feeling "rushed" and "hurried" all the time. They want their parents to focus on them when they're together. Galinsky refers to this as "focused time" and "hang around time." Both are important to children and their parents, and I know this is true from conversations with various clients about their experiences growing up with working parents. It was the moments when they felt they received their parents' full attention that had an impact on and made a difference in their lives.

Once again, working reduced hours is an option that can lead to the best of both worlds—more relaxed time with your family, yet time to pursue and maintain a career.

Child Care Options for the Part-Time Professional

One of the biggest benefits for parents working part-time—apart from the great emotional boost of having more time for yourself and your family—is not having to deal with the cost and hassle of full-time child care.

Nevertheless, most part-time workers, including those working at home, need to make some child care arrangements for preschool children. I know people working out of their home who have attempted to wing it—working during nap times, preschool days, or mother's-day-out programs, but that gets dicey. What happens if your child doesn't want to take a nap and you have a project due? Or if your child is sick and can't go to preschool that day? If you go this route, make sure you have emergency backup for deadline days or that there's flexibility in your job to adjust to sick days.

If you work at home, you might choose to have in-home child care with a part-time nanny. The advantage of this arrangement is that your child has the babysitter's undivided attention. The disadvantage is that unless you enroll your child in extracurricular activities, it can be very isolating for both of them. Another disadvantage is the cost; one-on-one child care can be very expensive. Be prepared to pay a part-time nanny higher hourly wages than you would a full-time nanny. You may also need to offer benefits to attract quality help. Because of these and other issues, many women share child care with another parent. Sharing a nanny can work very well when you trust and communicate well with the other parent. This is particularly important when one of you needs to switch your assigned day. If you live close to one another and an emergency occurs, you can drop off your child at the other person's home. Your child will be more comfortable than being left with a stranger.

This arrangement is also advantageous for a babysitter working for two families, which can reduce burnout and boredom. The sitter can learn from the two families and develop great relationships with both. Furthermore, the babysitter is paid full-time.

A major disadvantage of sharing a sitter is if the families involved suddenly stop getting along. This could lead to stress for the children as well as the parents. The key to success for this type of arrangement is flexibility and trust between both families.

You can also find a way to "job share" child care with another part-time working parent in your vicinity. For example, you watch your neighbor's children Monday and Friday morning, and she watches your children Tuesday and Wednesday afternoons. In fact, it's a good idea to create a network of working parents who can assist one another during a crisis—whether it involves work or home.

Another child care option is using pre- and after-school programs. There are also weeklong camps available during vacation breaks.

Day care is another alternative. I recommend that you visit the day care center and get recommendations from other parents who use it. I know individuals who work part-time and arrange day care for only two full days a week. This gives them focused work time on those days when the child is out of the home.

TIPS

- To ensure that your child is receiving attention, check in with him or her during the day, regardless of the child's age.
- To avoid feeling guilty when you're at work, you need to have a clear understanding why you need and/or want to work and remind yourself of those reasons during the day.
- Be prepared to make adjustments as your children grow and their needs change. The sitter who was perfect for a toddler may be too laid back for an active school-age child.

FURTHER RESOURCES

- Child Care Resource Center, www.ccrcinc.org
- www.childcare.org
- www.childcareaware.org
- www.childcarecanada.org
- www.childcareresourcesinc.org
- National Association of Child Care Resources and Referral Agencies, www.naccrra.org
- National Association for Family Child Care, www.nafcc.org

Making the Move: Small Steps

Whether you're moving out from a full-time position to a part-time one or moving from homemaking to the work world, I advise taking small steps. It will be awkward at first, but keep on going. Every bit of movement helps whether you're able to sense it or not. Do you know why babies take a long time learning to walk? It's because walking is really a process of catching yourself when you are about to fall down. The key is to lift one foot and then the other. You'll feel comfortable with your work situation eventually.

Build momentum; your first few months will feel awkward as you try to balance work and family. Fulfillment and awareness do not happen instantly; each action builds on itself. Every step along the way matters, and every bit of movement is a win, because, as I have said before, strength builds on strength.

Real-Life Examples

ENJOYING TIME OFF, WHETHER VOLUNTARY OR INVOLUNTARY

I know men who've lost their jobs because of downsizing. Once the initial shock and sadness had passed, some were able to reap the benefits of the time they now had to spend with their family. What they saw initially as an unfortunate event turned out to be a powerful experience in their lives. For the first time, these individuals were able to see the daily routine in the home and appreciate the effort that goes into running a home and a family.

One individual with whom I worked had a wonderful experience. For the time he was out of work, he enrolled in a class with his young daughter. He looked forward to this every week. He bonded with her, and the benefits to him and his family were great. He's now back at work, and although he enjoys his job and is doing well financially, he finds he no longer has much time at home.

There's usually a silver lining in what appears to be a black cloud. When you're out of work and facing transition, try to appreciate the extra time you have for your personal needs and your family. Although it can be hard, especially if you're under financial stress, it can be a time of exploration and self-discovery. It's also usually short-lived, as most people eventually find other employment, so I try very hard to work with my clients to help them see the hidden benefits of a "job break."

INTERVIEW WITH A WRITER

An interview with a writer revealed the challenges of parenting and work. She worked full-time initially, and she and her husband balanced their work schedules so that someone would always be home with the children. They were a true team. After their first child, they had twins.

When the twins were born, the wife reduced her schedule to four days a week with child care at home. She was working on a script, and it was very intense. She found it difficult to catch up at home after a stressful four-day workweek, and she felt guilty not being able to accomplish what she needed to at work. It was not a satisfying experience for her. It must be said, however, that some jobs would be impossible and stressful even if a person worked forty, fifty, or sixty hours a week! Ultimately, she had to face the fact that a reduced schedule didn't fit her particular job.

Now she has found something that works better for her. She's writing a play and trying to drum up interest in and support for it. Recently, she turned down a full-time job offer in her line of work that was a terrific opportunity, because she felt it was not appropriate for her at this time. She's doing two things now—taking a creative risk to fulfill a longtime passion and spending more quality time with her children.

Her tips for balancing work and family:

- Arrange good, dependable child care. This is especially challenging and difficult to find when the children get older, since they need someone to help with their schoolwork.
- Get organized. She considers herself the "CEO" of the family. Small things help—she keeps her shopping list on a computer program to speed up that routine task.
- Work on good communication with your partner, so you can pick up one another's slack.
- Lower your expectations. For example, your children might not be able to attend every activity and play date they want, and you may not be able to attend every activity and meeting that you want!
- See the positives. For the writer, one of the key benefits of being a working mother is that her kids see their mom working. She can be a very helpful role model.

INTERVIEW WITH A SENIOR WALL STREET ANALYST

For five years, this woman worked for an "amazing" boss. She got her employer to extend her maternity leave from three months to six, and when it was time for her to return, she decided she only wanted to work two days a week and the company agreed. She did not receive benefits because employees at that particular company have to work thirty hours a week to qualify for benefits.

For the next two and a half years, she worked Tuesdays and Thursdays and absolutely loved it. She had ample time to take her son to classes, join play groups, and "hang out" with him. She felt respected at the firm and worked very hard to earn that respect. On occasion, she stayed late and worked at home and was flexible when the situation required her to work longer hours. While she was working, her life was effectively balanced.

However, a new boss changed all that, and her position ended. She didn't give up; she and a co-worker proposed a job share. They knew one another and the job requirements very well. At the last minute, the firm got scared and said no.

At present, she is not working, and she misses the challenges and stimulation of working as a professional very much. It's hard when you have a great situation and then lose it. The moral of this story is that it takes work, trial and error, and repeated attempts to find the right position. Don't give up.

INTERVIEW WITH A PODIATRIST

The podiatrist I interviewed decided to go from full-time to part-time when her children were twenty, seventeen, and fifteen. At first glance, this may seem unusual, as many parents opt to work part-time during the preschool years. However, she felt that her children needed her time and attention more as teenagers than they did as small children.

Her schedule is three full days and two half-days. Since she's her own boss, she is also able to schedule personal appointments around her work. Her children take pride in her profession, and it's a great outlet for her. Her biggest challenge is financial, but she feels the sacrifices are worth the extra time she's created to focus on her children.

She originally selected podiatry as a specialty because she thought it was a good choice for both parenting and work, since the profession doesn't entail a lot of after-hour emergencies. From her perspective, it's actually harder to stay home all day. On Mondays, she is sometimes relieved to go to the office. Especially as the children get older, she feels parenting can be emotionally exhausting work, and her professional practice becomes a buffer for stress.

INTERVIEW WITH A SENIOR ASSOCIATE AT A NEW YORK LAW FIRM

The senior associate decided to work part-time after her maternity leave, and her firm agreed because she was an associate in good standing. Now she works three days at the office and one day at home. With her BlackBerry and other office technology, she always feels connected and involved. She would prefer to work at home two days a week, but the company hasn't agreed to that proposition.

She believes her high-paying job makes her life easier, as she's able to pay for quality help, vacations, dinners out, and other leisure activities. If she didn't work, this lifestyle wouldn't be possible. Of course, not everyone wants or needs to finance an expensive lifestyle; this is her choice.

The advantage of working for a large firm is that the company isn't entirely dependent on her. She also finds it very rewarding to have time away from the home and to be involved with activities outside the school and community. The ability to have a work life and a personal life helps her buffer the stress in both arenas.

The greatest challenges for her include keeping up with the work since the law changes all the time. Another challenge is finding the right nanny who understands what she wants for her kids. Her priority is the children, and she prides herself on the fact that she hasn't missed one important event. If necessary, she shifts her schedule around to be there for them.

Her firm does have an alternative work schedule, but only

nine out of two hundred associates take advantage of it. She realizes her decision has taken her off the partnership track, but that's not what's most important to her.

INTERVIEW WITH A PART-TIME WORKING DAD

This part-time working dad balances many passions and activities. He's a writer and an editor and teaches a university course in the evening and a novel workshop out of his home. He decided to take care of his two young daughters while his wife pursues her career at a bank, a position that involves a great deal of travel.

He has embraced his role wholeheartedly. By the time his wife arrives home, he has cooked dinner and the children have been fed. He values the fact that he's been able to focus on his daughters and is astounded when he accompanies his wife to conferences and hear other men brag that they never spend much time with their children.

His choice is not without challenges, however. The isolation of being at home is one. His initial attempts to join playgroups failed. Many of the moms used the time for "gal talk," including "ragging" on their husbands. They certainly didn't want a male presence. Eventually, he found a playgroup that accepted him, and he said it "saved his life." He greatly appreciated the camaraderie and shared information, and the members have all become close friends.

He finds that the other stay-at-home dads he runs into aren't nearly as good at forming such alliances. They don't share information and generally send out a "leave me alone" message.

The greatest challenge for him is the difficulty of feeling successful based on the concept of success in America—money. For example, when he applied for an after-school program, he felt he needed to defend his life and work.

At present, he continues to teach and edit manuscripts; however, he's frustrated because he doesn't have much time for writing, which is his passion. He needs a chunk of time, ten hours to write and concentrate, and right now, with balancing work and kids, this isn't possible, which leaves him with feelings of profound guilt. His wife feels the same way; having it all is very difficult.

RESOURCES:

- www.bluesuitmom.com; offers tips for managing family, careers, money, time, health, food, etc.
- www.catalystwomen.org; a research and advisory organization working with business and the professions to build inclusive environments and expand opportunities for women at work
- Entrepreneurial Mothers Association, www.emausa.org ; professional and personal development for self-employed mothers
- National Family and Parenting Institute, www.e-parents.org; a UK site that advocates for a family-friendly society, offers tips and resources
- Families and Work Institute, www.familiesandwork.org; provides research and data on work/family issues
- www.fathersdirect.com; a UK site with extensive information and resources
- www.fatherworld.com; resources for fathers at home
- *The Job/Family Challenge: A 9 to 5 Guide: Not for Women Only* by Ellen Bravo (Wiley, 1995).
- www.laborproject.org; the Labor Project for Working Families partners with unions to put families first.
- *Maternity Leave: The Working Woman's Practical Guide to Combining Pregnancy, Motherhood and Career* by Eileen L. Casey (Green Mountain, 1992).
- www.mommyenterprises.com; tips and resources for those who want to work at home
- www.momsrefuge.com; family and career resources for mothers
- *Now What Do I Do? The Woman's Guide to a New Career* by Jan Cannon, Ph.D. (Capital Books, 2005)

- www.parenting.com; includes a "work and family" section
- www.mothersandmore.org; resources and links, an action and advocacy section
- The National Partnership for Women and Families, www.nationalpartnership.org; promotes fairness in the workplace and policies that help parents balance work and family
- Alfred P. Sloan Foundation, www.sloan.org; provides links to research on family work/life balance and workplace flexibility issues
- *The Three-Career Couple: Her Job, His Job & Their Job Together: Mastering the Fine Art of Juggling Work, Home, and Family* by Marcia Byalick and Linda Saslow (Peterson's, 1993).
- Work At Home Moms, www.wahm.com; resources and links
- www.workfamily.com; a clearinghouse for work-life information, including tips and resources for making your company more work-life friendly
- www.workingfamilies.org.uk; a UK site that helps children, working parents, and their employers find a better balance between responsibilities at home and at work
- University of California, Hastings College of Law, www.u chastings.edu/?pid = 3624; "aims to end employment discrimination against workers who have family responsibilities"
- www.workingmother.com; features, among other resources, "100 Best Companies for Working Mothers"

CHAPTER 8

Perfect for the Boomer Generation

President John F. Kennedy once famously declared that adding years to peoples' lives was not enough. "Our objective," he said, "might be to add new life to those years." Those words seem even more relevant today as we see longer life spans, earlier retirements, better health, and higher costs of living than ever before. Couple those facts with looming deficits in Social Security, pensions, and personal savings, and you can understand the twofold scenario facing this country's aging baby boomers: many people will *need to work* and *want to work* in their retirement years.

Fortunately, most seniors and aging baby boomers won't have to work full-time to finance the lifestyles to which they've become accustomed. After all, they've paid their nose-to-the-grindstone dues, and now they want fulfilling work that cushions the bank account and keeps them active and involved mentally, physically, socially, and emotionally.

This makes part-time work an ideal situation. This chapter describes the benefits of working part-time and provides concrete and practical tips for finding the best part-time position.

The Need to Work: Money Matters

Life expectancy rose from forty-seven years to seventy-seven in the twentieth century and is likely to rise to one hundred in the twenty-first century. This means that many people will need more money over a longer period. It appears unlikely that most will have enough in pensions, personal savings, and Social Security to sustain them. Why? Because pensions are disappearing or being replaced by 401(k) plans in which the recipients, not the employers, bear the investment risks. Personal savings are hard to accrue due to the high cost of living, and the future of Social Security by all accounts is in jeopardy.

As a result, many aging workers who had expected to ease comfortably out of the labor force in their fifties and early sixties are discovering that they don't have the financial resources to support themselves comfortably throughout a long retirement. This means people over age fifty-five will most likely continue working. However, this doesn't have to be a bleak work-until-you-die prospect. Part-time employment lets you address financial needs in a balanced way while providing the health and emotional benefits of an active life.

Pensions and 401(k) Plans

According to Barbara McIntosh, chair of the National Older Worker Employment Partnership, only 50 percent of current U.S. workers have pension plans and, among those, pensions are diminishing. For example, a major airline recently cut union members' pensions by more than half. Other large industries appear to face a similar pension plan crisis. Katherine Stone, a professor of employment law at the UCLA School of Law, writes in a 2005 *Washington Post* article, "The Retirement You Weren't Banking On," that such pension-slashing actions "may well mark the beginning of the end of the system of retirement planning as we know it." Such actions, "more than the predicted short-fall of Social Security decades from now, will have a real impact on the retirement of real people who live in real time." Stone cautions that such changes to pension plans "should send shivers up your spine."

Personal Savings

Personal savings plans require the young to look into the future and decide how much of their finances to allocate. This is very difficult for younger people to do; inevitably, they do not set aside enough.

Older people are concerned about how their children and grandchildren will get by in old age. They feel that the young spend too much money and don't save enough. Many will not have much left for a comfortable retirement; their last resort will be to sell their homes to make up for the lack of retirement funds.

The best course of action is to educate people about the importance of personal savings. The next course of action is to make sure people understand that their need to work will increase during their life span, which is precisely why you need to do proper career and retirement planning at specific stages in life.

Social Security

The previous generation of retirees had a large population of well-educated people with good jobs to finance their retirement. Now, as a large crop of baby boomers with extended life expectancies moves toward retirement, there are fewer people in the workforce to finance the safety net of Social Security.

People can currently retire at sixty-two and take early benefits or wait until the full retirement age of sixty-six to start collecting. However, the benefits are substantially lower at age sixty-two. Either way, if you thought Social Security alone will see you comfortably or even adequately through an extended life, think again.

Barbara McIntosh, chair of National Older Workers Employment Partnership says in a 2005 *Vermont Quarterly* interview that Social Security may not be available at all for younger baby boomers. She adds that, with the way things are going, Social Security is predicted to be out of funds by 2047. That's a stern warning given that 20 percent of retirees currently rely on Social Security as their sole source of income, and 65 percent of seniors count on it for half their money. Other calculations state that between 2037 and 2075, the Social Security program is projected to run annual deficits totaling 30 trillion dollars (justfacts.com/socialsecurity.htm).

To salvage Social Security, there is talk of raising the retirement age, reducing benefit costs, and increasing taxes paid by workers on the job. In any event, it's never too late to start investigating and planning. Certainly, if you're nearing retirement age, consult a financial planner or a Social Security representative on the best time to retire to get the maximum benefits.

Health Care Coverage and Medicare

Fewer large private companies offer current and future retirees health benefits, according to a 2005 *New York Times* article, "Health Coverage Dispute Pits Older Retirees Against Younger." In addition, many are anticipating the same trend in the public sector, as reported in the *New York Times* article, "The Next Retirement Bomb." The problem is exacerbated in the public sector because many individuals forfeited higher salaries to collect better retirement benefits. Many will suffer greatly since they don't have a lot of time to make up for this gap. These public and private sector trends mean that many will need to work solely to receive health benefits.

Medicare is available at age sixty-five; however, Medicare will not pay for all your health needs. It limits the types of services it pays, and there can be very high co-payments and deductibles. In addition, the program is only available if you are at least sixty-five years of age and contributed to Social Security for a minimum of ten years, or if you bought into Medicare (source: elderhelpline.org).

FURTHER RESOURCES
- AARP, aarp.org, features a "best" list of companies for

people over fifty and employers that offer benefits, including health benefits

- See chapter 6 for a partial list of companies that offer health benefits to find the directories that will link you to companies so you can search for information on benefits, and for more "best companies" to work for lists, as these companies often include benefits.

The Desire to Work

It's not all doom and gloom. People may *need* to work to provide adequate support, but the good news is that most seniors *want* to work at some level. According to Ken Dychtwald, a consultant on aging, the golden years of retirement were well received by those born between 1900 and 1945, but baby boomers are changing that perspective. Retirement is no longer viewed as an endless vacation. There's a widespread belief now that too much leisure can be boring.

Survey after survey bears this out. AARP (formerly the American Association of Retired Persons) found that 80 percent of baby boomers plan to do some sort of work into their seventies. Likewise, a 2005 Merrill Lynch retirement survey found that baby boomers will create a "new model of retirement" by alternating work and leisure. According to that survey, 65 percent plan to retire from their current full-time jobs and launch entirely new part-time careers, endeavors that are more in line with their values and lifestyle choices.

There was a massive study of emerging attitudes about aging, maturity, and retirement from around the globe, called "The Future of Retirement." The surprising finding was that throughout the world people don't want to be judged by their age alone but by their energy, attitude, and what they are making of their life. Forget the "golden years" model of a slow fade into the sunset. Instead, a new perspective has emerged that focuses on new beginnings and personal change. Becoming aware that we can have new experiences and new careers can inspire us and reduce our fear that getting older means being out of touch.

Furthermore, the survey asked elders around the world what they believed contributed most to a healthy and positive old age. The three most frequent answers were: family and friends, maintaining health, and financial preparedness. I would add a fourth—trying something you haven't done before, including working part-time in an area of interest.

The Benefits of Staying Active

As a healthier, better-educated, and longer-living generation, we are going to want and need continued challenges and mental stimulation. There are so many benefits to working part-time. In the last section, we discussed the financial rewards. Now we discuss the physical, mental, emotional, and social aspects as well.

When I was a child in grade school, I distinctly remember the teacher emphasizing that good health includes your physical, mental, emotional, and social well-being. To this day, I still refer to these four factors.

PHYSICAL BENEFITS

Retiring too early may be bad for your health. Although the nation's Social Security system is set up for a "usual" retirement age of sixty-five, some analysts warn that able-bodied men and women in their sixties may be retiring too early with costs to them as well as society. Many people, for example, experience a rapid decline in physical and mental health soon after retirement, often due to lack of activity and purpose. Marital strain can also develop if one or both people hang around the house with too much idle time and not enough stimulation ("The Able-bodied Retiree Doesn't Need Our Help," *USA Today*).

There's much anecdotal evidence of this phenomenon. How many times have you heard a story about someone's health deteriorating as soon as he or she retires? There's a growing belief that those who keep working live longer, and that inactivity can be hazardous to your health. Sociologists, on the other hand, say it's a bit more complicated than that. I, and others, believe the key is to enjoy the work that you do to sustain longevity and the desire to work.

In Guang Xi, Southwest China, is a world-famous longevity hometown known as Bama Yao Autonomous Country. According to a 1997 survey, among the country's 230,000 inhabitants, there were eighty-one people over one hundred years old, and 226 people between the ages of ninety and ninety-five; the oldest person was 130.

It's a very mountainous area, and the physical exercise required, coupled with a lifetime of hard work, has given these people strong muscles and bones, thought to be one reason for their long life span. Centenarians in the town, however, believe the secret of longevity is to do good deeds, help others, be kind, have confidence, and never give up ("Looking for the Secret of Longevity," *Travel China*).

MENTAL BENEFITS

Staying mentally alert is key, and the more complex the task for doing so, the better. As a result, many older adults try to learn a new language or musical instrument later in life. The benefits can be enormous. A National Institute of Mental Health study concluded that "complex work increases intellectual flexibility." In fact, the effect is found to be "significantly greater" for older workers than for younger ones ("When to Hold, When to Fold," *New York Times*).

In his last op-ed column in the *New York Times*, editorialist William Safire notes that we are living longer, but asks the question: "To what purpose? Extending the life of the body gains most meaning when preserving the life of the mind."

He advises readers to think about a longevity strategy. He says he received the following counsel: never retire; you can change your career but make sure whatever you do keeps your "synapses snapping." He further states that fresh stimulation is what all of us should require in "the last of life." He's taking his own advice—he's retiring as an editorialist but continuing at the Charles A. Dana Foundation, where he will help to form the Dana Alliance for Brain Initiatives.

EMOTIONAL BENEFITS

Hitting the half-century mark is a big deal, physically and emotionally. There's often a sense of uncertainty and disequilibrium, a sense of loss, as we get older. We're going through a time of change. We need to face the change and feel the loss; acknowledging this allows us to better cope with our feelings.

In a segment on the *Today Show*, "Why 50 Is the New 30," Dr. Thomas Perls, a professor of geriatrics at Boston University Medical Center, and Judy Turner, a psychologist with the Mid-Life Institute in Toronto, discussed how men and women age differently.

While women experience more physical and hormonal changes, they're also more likely to use aging as an opportunity for reassessment, asking what they want out of life, where they're going, and how they want to spend their time and energy. Men, on the other hand, tend to respond to the external ramifications and see only the losses—the younger colleagues who get the promotions or, worse yet, losing jobs to younger workers. The result is depression.

It would be helpful if there were more education in our society around the emotional changes that men and women experience and greater acceptance of the aging process. This would heighten the opportunity for all of us to engage in re-evaluation and growth at this stage in our lives.

SOCIAL BENEFITS

Work also provides an important social outlet. For some, it is like having a family. Many jobs are very social in nature, for example, retail and customer service. Such jobs provide a way for older people to remain out in the world and interact. In addition, work gives structure to our lives and helps to organize our day.

The Need for Older Workers:
The Looming Labor Shortage

It's not just about seniors needing to work or wanting to work; our society and economy need them to work as well. Consider this: there are approximately seventy-six to seventy-eight million baby boomers (those between the ages of forty-one and fifty-nine) in the United States. When they "retire," there will be large gaps in the workforce, not just in numbers, but also in brainpower and experience.

These predicted labor shortages have a positive side for seniors because they will have more power to negotiate flexible work arrangements that suit their "golden years" needs.

Barbara McIntosh, chair of the National Older Worker Employment Partnership, says in an article in *Vermont Quarterly*, "According to the Bureau of Labor Statistics, the pool of workers ages 35 to 44 will shrink by 7 percent between 2002 and 2012. Employers will need to make a much greater effort to retain their older, experienced workers."

According to the *Wall Street Journal*, some companies that fear a labor exodus are already developing programs to cater to older workers. For example, some companies are letting employees "technically retire" but remain involved on a contractual basis. For example, IBM employs retirees to work on special projects and to share their experience with younger workers.

Other companies, such as Home Depot, have gotten involved with AARP to recruit older workers, many of whom were laid off by other companies. As an added bonus, Hope Depot offers health insurance to part-timers.

FURTHER RESOURCES
- See the "featured employers" link in the "money and work" section of aarp.org.
- The Alliance for an Experienced Workforce, experienced workforce.org, helps employers engage and use the skills of those over fifty.

A BOOST TO THE ECONOMY

Having seniors in the workforce earning money, paying taxes, then spending that money and putting it back into the marketplace will clearly be a boost to the economy. Having seniors supplement their income and pay more taxes also lessens the burden on the younger generation in terms of financing Social Security and Medicare.

According to a 2005 *BusinessWeek* cover story on retirement, "Old. Smart. Productive," "Increased productivity of older Americans and higher labor-force participation could add 9% to gross domestic product by 2045"—a percentage that amounts to "$3 trillion a year, in today's dollars."

There's another psychological plus to this situation. If you ever feel bad or guilty about spending money, think of it this way: you're doing your part to keep the economy healthy.

LAWSUIT VICTORY ON AGE DISCRIMINATION OPENS DOORS

Age discrimination definitely exists—study after study proves this, and none other than the Supreme Court has backed that finding in a recent decision (*General Dynamics Land Systems, Inc. v. Cline*) that makes it easier for seniors to sue for age discrimination. The ruling allows older workers to use the same kind of proof as victims of race or sex discrimination. Now in-house lawyers are warning their companies to reevaluate their treatment of older workers regarding promotions and layoffs.

This is a clear wake-up call to companies, and one that is needed in view of the looming labor shortages. It's a win-win situation for everyone, because employers benefit by being forced to shake off stereotypes and prejudices, since older workers are often the most competent and conscientious.

Positive Attributes of Older Workers

OLDER WORKERS ARE DEPENDABLE

Older workers bring many positive attributes to the workplace.

According to AARP and the Employment Development Department of California (as reported in "A Positive Perspective on Aging, Planning, and Adult Development," from a speech to career development professionals by Howard Figler, *Career Network Newsletter*, 1992):

- Workers hired after age forty generally attain a higher average performance rating in a shorter time than do those hired before age thirty.
- Workers forty or older quit their jobs less than half as often as do younger workers.
- Older workers have better attendance and health and injury records than do younger workers.
- The number of days lost per workdays for all reasons decreases as age increases. Workers in every age group above fifty lost fewer scheduled workdays than those in younger age groups..

I can attest to this personally. For the past four years, I've had an assistant who was hired after the age of fifty, and she's been terrific. Her attendance record is impeccable. Because of her various life experiences, she is of great help to me in many areas, personally and professionally. Colleagues of mine have made similar decisions that have worked out well for them.

This was also confirmed recently in the *New York Times* article, "More Help Wanted: Older Workers Please Apply." After years of encouraging workers to take early retirement to cut jobs, a growing number of companies are hunting for older workers because they have lower turnover rates and, in many cases, better work performance. Some companies have even begun offering "snowbird specials"—winter work in Florida and summer work in Maine.

OLDER WORKERS ARE EXPERIENCED

It's not only dependability that counts. Experience is probably the greatest asset of older people. Today's older workforce is better educated than ever before. Add to that years of experience, and you have a resource that can't easily be topped by young, inexperienced people.

For example, the *Business Week* cover story reports, "Many highly educated and well-paid workers—lawyers, physicians, architects—already work to advanced ages because their skills are valued. Boomers, with more education than any generation in history, are likely to follow that pattern."

OLDER WORKERS HAVE BETTER PEOPLE SKILLS

Older workers can model social skills to younger staff. According to "A Generation Gap, a Workplace Chasm," in the *New York Times*, older employees have suggested to younger ones that instead of only trading email messages with customers, they should enclose an actual written note when they send out packages. This might not occur to a younger employer, yet many people appreciate the personal touch.

Despite the widespread belief that older workers resent a younger boss, many find that working with and for younger people is refreshing; it enriches their perspective.

OLDER WORKERS ARE LESS PRONE TO CONFLICT

According to Kira Birditt, a research fellow at the University of Michigan and lead author on two studies, older people experience less anger and less stress and use less aggressive strategies when they have problems in relationships.

In a study whose results appeared in May 2005 *The Journal of Gerontology: Psychological Sciences*, interviews were conducted with 184 people ages thirteen to ninety-nine to determine how they solve interpersonal problems. The conclusion was that people older than eighty were more likely to avoid conflict by waiting until things improved, while younger people often chose to leave in anger and engage in yelling and name calling. Studies also confirm that older adults of both sexes appear to be better at handling conflict, not only with family but also with co-workers, neighbors, and acquaintances.

It makes sense that after living through many interpersonal situations and conflicts, an older person has the wisdom and experience to put many issues in perspective. This research clearly dispels the notion that we become grumpier as we age. Interestingly, while confronting issues is often viewed as the best way to handle interpersonal problems, older adults often avoid this approach. Many believe others are unlikely to change, so why bother. I suppose one of my favorite expressions, "let it be," applies here.

MYTH BUSTING

- Seniors are bad at technology. Not true! According to several studies, while seniors may be slower to learn new technology, once they learn it, they tend to make fewer mistakes. To ease the intimidation factor some seniors feel when learning new technological skills, Barbara McIntosh suggests that companies have two training sessions. Moreover, according to the *BusinessWeek* article cited earlier, the rapid changeover in technology plays to seniors' favor in that it's just as easy to "retrain old employees as young ones."

- Seniors aren't creative. Not true! *BusinessWeek* details university research that found that the "innovations of older people are more likely to be 'experimental,' vs. the break the mold 'conceptual' innovations of younger types." There are plenty of examples of people who became very successful when others might have considered them over the hill. For example, Theodore Geisel published his first Dr. Seuss book at age fifty, and Ray Kroc opened the first McDonald's restaurant when he was fifty-three.

- Seniors aren't physically or mentally up to challenges. Not true! Better health care, better diets, advanced technology, a diminished reliance on physical labor, and memory-enhancing medicines are all helping to keep seniors top-notch employees long after typical retirement years. And if everyone followed medical advice on diet and exercise, we'd be doing our part not just to increase the length of our lives but, more important, their quality as well.

In the past, companies haven't always been fair in offering training programs to older workers. Instead, they've given training and education to the young. Recent rulings on age discrimination, combined with labor shortages, should help put an end to this unfair and unproductive practice.

Tips for Seniors to Make Themselves More Marketable When Looking for Work

- Network all the time. Attend events, parties, association meetings, etc., anything that gets you out with people. Practice beforehand a two-minute pitch to communicate and let people know you're looking for a part-time position.
- Keep your computer skills current. Classes are available through local adult education programs and at community colleges, senior centers, and other civic organizations. Having the ability to work with major software programs, databases, and presentation applications keeps you current and is always appreciated in the marketplace.
- Stay active. Take classes in any area of interest. Volunteer. Every experience you have is a resource for networking and building your contacts.
- Search out employers who value older workers (check out the "Best Employers for People Over 50" on aarp.org and consult other links to "best of employers" listed in chapter 6).
- Keep a young state of mind; don't focus on your age.

Tips for Older Workers on Job Interviews

Older job hunters can overcome prejudice through positive thinking and being direct and confident with interviewers; this is the same advice I would offer anyone in a job search. The key is to look sharp and be enthusiastic. Emphasize your strong interest in doing the job well and highlight your value to the organization using specific examples (applicable experience, people skills, dependability, maturity).

Don't be surprised if a younger person interviews you and does not treat you with as much respect as you would like. Older workers often feel they deserve more respect from younger colleagues than they receive. This might not happen. The interviewer might keep you waiting or might not fully appreciate all of your accomplishments.

Despite this, if you're interested in the position, you must make the best possible presentation in each interview. For example, everyone you meet is important, and the slightest hesitancy of one interviewer can jeopardize your chance of obtaining the desired position. The first person interviewing you might only be doing the initial screening. If you show any disrespect or have a bad attitude, you may be doing yourself a disservice. You want to stay focused on the job opening, your abilities and accomplishments, and why you want the job. Try to mention your most recent and relevant accomplishments. I recommend keeping your resume as current as possible; it's often a good idea to consider eliminating jobs that go back to the beginning of your employment years.

Draw up a list of questions you might be asked and prepare possible answers. Always be prepared to answer any questions that may apply to older workers. Some examples of tricky questions you might encounter:

- Aren't you used to making more money? Possible answer: My financial needs are taken care of, and I can afford to take this job.
- Aren't you overqualified? Is this going to be challenging enough? Possible answer: I love new experiences, and this will allow me to use different skills from those I've used before.
- Can you work for a younger boss? Possible answer: I appreciate youth for their ideas and energy.

Personality Styles and Retirement

Some may ask, "When can I simply retire and have little or no responsibility? I don't want to keep working." I believe it's a very personal situation. Those who study aging say that many people's patterns of behavior usually do not change just because they get older. From my experience working with people in career and life planning, it's usually predictable who will do what when they age. Individuals who have had an interest in travel will travel. Those who have been philanthropic may choose to take on a more active role in that area. Those who were physically active will exercise more. Doers will continue "doing," and risk takers will continue risk taking. If work was central in your life, and you gained great satisfaction from that, you'll need to find something to satisfy that need as you age.

Making the Decision to Retire

Making any transition is difficult, but deciding to alter your life by changing your career or the amount of time you devote to it can cause considerable stress. If you're considering retirement, here is a list of questions to consider:

- Will you feel comfortable financially without a regular income?
- Will you have interests that you can see yourself spending time on or expanding if you retire?
- Are there new areas of interest you would like to pursue?
- Do you have adequate resources within the community that you can draw on if you choose to retire—religious affiliations, clubs, community activities, etc.?
- Do you have friends who have retired or other people with whom you socialize regularly?
- If you live with someone, is your partner or spouse in agreement regarding your retirement?

- When you worked, what did you get out of the experience? Was it solely financial? A mental challenge? A social outlet? You need to have adequate replacements if you choose to retire.

These questions should help you gauge your readiness for retirement. If you are energized by accomplishing things on a regular basis, you need to think through your decision to retire carefully. Furthermore, if you like structure and being on a schedule, retirement may not be for you. Part-time work options might be the best course to consider, as they can help ease you into full retirement.

Tips for Dealing with the Stress and Uncertainty of Change

Change is exciting *and* scary. For those who like things to be black and white, this can be a very challenging time. Here are some guidelines to ease you through the transition:

- Accept where you are now and don't fight it.
- Set clear, manageable short-term goals.
- Manage financial stressors to the best of your ability.
- Surround yourself with supportive people.
- Create a "board of directors" for advice and direction: doctor, CPA, attorney, friends, family, etc. Your inner circle can serve as a rich resource for specific advice and feedback.

Real-Life Example: Business Owner

A restaurant owner decided to retire after he sold his business. Three months later he gained a great deal of weight and found himself becoming very anxious at home. His wife worked a long day, and he did not enjoy being home alone.

The retiree's accountant knew he was restless. When the accountant heard of a neighborhood pizza restaurant for sale, he told his client about it. The former restaurant owner was interested. Despite the weight gain, he was in good health and agile. After some contemplation, he realized retirement wasn't for him, and he bought the establishment.

Since buying the restaurant, his energy has improved. He is thrilled with his new venture. Because it's close to his home, he has a short commute. He arrives in the morning, leaves for a few hours in the afternoon, and returns later in the day. To speak with this man, you can hear his satisfaction with his new business. He loves the customers and takes great pride in his restaurant. He told me this makes him very happy; especially since he was miserable at home when he retired.

He had worked throughout his life; not working was unbearable. According to him, work is like vitamins, it keeps him healthy. I frequent his pizzeria often and always see him socializing with the customers and tending to their needs. He's always smiling. He also enjoys the back office work. This man clearly made a good decision.

Options for Part-Time Work

I discussed the various options for working part-time in chapter 4, how to negotiate for part-time work in chapter 5, and how to find part-time work in chapter 6. All of those apply to seniors, but I focus on some other senior-specific information here.

PHASED-IN OR GRADUAL RETIREMENT

Phased-in or gradual retirement is becoming popular in today's work world and is likely to grow in popularity. This practice has many advantages:

- It allows companies to retain experienced workers who might choose complete retirement over endless days and hours in the office.
- It keeps experienced mentors on board to help train up-and-coming talent.

- It helps employees and management restructure smoothly and efficiently.
- It reduces office-related stress and the fear associated with rapid change and loss.
- It offers a good work/life benefit that helps to attract and retain employees

JOB SHARING

Many professional jobs are viewed as full-time endeavors. To get around this, you might want to propose a job share (see chapters 4 and 5 for specific tips and resources on job sharing). There are many benefits to the employer in this arrangement: the position is always covered, two sets of skills are better than one, and you—the senior employee—are training someone to take over when you leave.

The most challenging part of a job share is finding the right person to work with you. At the same time, many people would love to find a quality job share, for example, parents, people reentering the workplace, other seniors, and those seeking a reduced schedule for personal reasons, to name a few.

TAKE A RISK: START THE BUSINESS OF YOUR DREAMS

Instead of retiring, some are taking the opportunity to transfer their skills to building a business they have always dreamed of. I once heard of a therapist who remarked, "Every executive I know dreams of opening a hot dog stand on the beach." Your dream may not be a hot dog stand, but you get the point. If you've reached a time in your life when your major financial considerations are taken care of, why not take some risks. Do what you want while your health is good and you have the energy to do so.

When you're older, it's increasingly important to do what you love. I believe the best situation to find yourself in is one that can draw on your wisdom, inspiration, personal experiences, and skills. How do you choose what business to go into? Choose one that matches your interests, motivated skills, and values (see chapter 3 for detailed information on personality types, value and skill assessments, and steps to career success and chapter 4 for tips and resources on starting your own business).

INDEPENDENT CONSULTANT

Becoming a consultant is an excellent option and a good fit for senior executives who have reached the end of corporate employment but still have the background and experience and the business network and clientele to make this endeavor very profitable.

In fact, a 2002 AARP study found that 16.4 percent of workers fifty and over were self-employed, and that one-third of them made that transition after fifty ("The New Golden Age," entrepreneur.com).

A 2002 survey by the Independent Direction Advisory Service, www.iddas.com, concluded that for executives who made the move to part-time careers, including working as independent consultants, money wasn't the prime motivator. Many were more interested in satisfaction, flexibility, and choice, and most were happy to be in control of their lives and free of office politics. The majority, 65 percent, said they were very satisfied or satisfied with their success at establishing an independent career, and many would not go back to corporate life if given the opportunity.

The study included suggestions for those considering the move to independent consultant:

- Start planning early.
- Speak to as many people as possible who have made a similar shift.
- Learn as much as you can about the market and trends.
- Attend the appropriate classes and conferences.
- Consider working with a coach to guide your independent career; take assessment tests, and talk about your strengths and weaknesses and where your skills might be of most value.
- Network.

- Do lots of self-marketing.
- Have financial reserves initially.

The potential disadvantages of becoming an independent consultant include finding consistent work, financial ups and downs, and loss of camaraderie. The last one, the potential isolation of working independently, is precisely why I recommend that professionals get involved in related organizations and associations.

Freelancing can also be a fun way to pursue longtime dreams, hobbies, and passions: writing, photography, art, collecting and selling, knitting, woodworking, etc. The list goes on and on. Pursuing your hobbies as a business also has the happy by-product of creating a social network of people who share your passions.

ADDITIONAL IDEAS FOR PROFESSIONAL PART-TIME POSITIONS

Chapters 4 and 6 have extensive information on options for part-time positions and how to find them, but here are some that are particularly suited to seniors or those about to enter the ranks:

- Smaller firms often have more flexible human resource plans, whereas larger firms often have layers of bureaucracy and ironclad job descriptions (see chapter 5 for information on how to negotiate a part-time position). Experience in and connections to an industry are welcome anywhere, but especially at smaller firms.
- Universities, hospitals, libraries, and other nonprofit organizations have a variety of interesting and interest-related part-time positions. Whenever I visit a library, it seems I see seniors happily working there. Remember that volunteer positions often lead to paid ones.
- Check federal, state, and local government opportunities. Many offer benefits packages for part-time employees.

- Don't want to leave home? Consider a computer-related business such as designing Web sites or managing an online business. Have you heard of virtual assistants? They provide support via fax, phone, computer, and the Internet. For more information, refer to the International Virtual Assistant Association, www.ivaa.org or www.virtual assistants.com.

- Good at selling? These positions are always in demand—the money potential is often good, and the hours are usually flexible. Consider anything from selling cars to real estate. Sellers need to be self-motivated, patient, and persuasive and have thick skins. If you weren't good at selling before—don't automatically turn up your nose. Age gives you experience and perspective. Remember, when you're over fifty and semi-retired, you can wear the color purple and not have to answer to anyone if you don't want to. One caveat: with any sales-related endeavor, make sure the organization is legitimate.

- Arbiter/mediator. This is a field where experience and life's accumulated wisdom are a must. For more information about beginning a career in mediation, visit www.mediate.com.

- Adjunct instructor or substitute teacher. The money isn't great, but these positions can be very rewarding. They provide a great way to share your knowledge and expertise and stay in touch with the younger generation. The demand is high, and some universities and school districts offer incentives and/or benefits.

- Health care workers are always in demand at hospitals and other care facilities, but insurance companies also employ doctors as consultants.

HOURLY WAGE EMPLOYMENT

You may also decide to choose a new, less demanding occupation. The money's not as good, but on the plus side, there is less stress, you won't have as many responsibilities, and it's easier to detach yourself. Many companies in the service industry are looking for hourly wage employees, including Home Depot, CVS, and many other retail establishments. There is an especially high demand for part-time employees at holiday time. I know women and men who started working in retail at an older age for the camaraderie as well as additional income. Being out in the world helping and speaking with many different types of people can be a real boost.

You might consider telemarketing or telefundraising. I know, I know—telemarketing doesn't sound appealing, but if you follow your interests, you can have a whole different attitude toward the experience. For example, many arts organizations look for telemarketers to sell subscriptions to the theater, ballet, and opera, and many nonprofit organizations conduct fundraising campaigns for the benefit of the environment, animals, children, the homeless, etc. The hourly wages for strictly commercial ventures are relatively high, and shifts are flexible; you can also work from home. Some salaries include commissions.

CRUISE FOR (ALMOST) FREE

How's this for a fun idea? Put your background and experience to use by becoming a lecturer or instructor on a cruise line. You usually aren't paid, but you do get free transportation, room and board, and entertainment. You can apply to a cruise line directly or work through an agency.

Agencies are looking for well-informed and personable speakers who can present entertaining and informative lectures to passengers. Lectures cover a wide range of fields, including but not limited to travel, history, animal studies, and art. Cruise companies also need dance instructors, hosts, and bridge directors. The benefits of working on a cruise ship are many: travel, entertainment, good food, and the chance to meet and interact with a wide range of people. Booking agencies in search of lecturers include:

- www.cruiselinejobs.com
- www.cruiseplacement.com
- www.shipjobs.com

- To Sea With Z, www.toseawithz.com
- www.theworkingvacation.com

Note: There are placement fees, and you need to evaluate whether the fee is worth it.

Volunteering as an "In" to Part-Time Work

Moving from a volunteer position to paid part-time work is a wonderful transitional opportunity. You eliminate many pieces of uncertainty because you already know the people and the routine of the organization.

REAL-LIFE EXAMPLES
FUNDRAISER AND VOLUNTEER COORDINATOR

I interviewed Vicki, who recently moved to a new area. The commute became too much for her, and she had to give up her former full-time position. She was fortunate not to have to work full-time; however, she felt she needed to do something. She found volunteer work to tide her over and to give her time to figure out what she wanted to do. Her volunteer experiences were all very pleasurable, so she told her supervisor that if anything came up, she would be interested in working part-time. Two years later, she was offered a three-day-a-week job.

She is now a project assistant in volunteer services at a major nonprofit organization, where she works with families in need. She feels she "stumbled" into a great position. She's making a difference in people's lives by fundraising and matching volunteers to people in need. At the end of the day, she goes home feeling good. She also has the added bonus of sharing her interests and value systems with her colleagues.

CANDIDATE FOR POLITICAL OFFICE

A woman I interviewed began her involvement in local politics as a volunteer in 1956, when she was at home raising four children. She called her local leader and expressed an interest and was encouraged to come to a meeting. Based on her enthusiasm, she was asked to become more involved. She joined the Democratic Party when few Democrats were being elected, and she helped build it up. Over the years she played various roles. She worked primaries; was appointed New York State Executive Committee representative; set up programs for the public on such issues as crime, drugs and gun control; and raised money for the U.S. Commission for the Preservation of America's Heritage Abroad.

Because she has been so successful in her past ventures, she was asked to run for Town Council. Currently in her midseventies, she will combine her earlier political involvement with this new challenge. She is a true role model for those who want to pursue their passions, at whatever age.

SCORE

If you want to strictly volunteer, I often recommend SCORE. The SCORE Association is a nonprofit association dedicated to entrepreneurial education and the formation, growth, and success of small businesses nationwide. As a retired professional, you can volunteer at SCORE and use your business expertise to provide confidential small-business advice to those who are just starting up.

SCORE has hundreds of offices nationwide. In addition, many volunteer counselors provide online counseling from offices and homes. Volunteers come from a variety of occupations and backgrounds: many owned small businesses for years, others worked for major firms. They share the belief that mentoring is a key component of success.

It is clearly a win-win situation for everyone. I know a man who needed some accounting help in his business. He contacted SCORE, and a retired accountant lent his expertise. Both enjoyed the relationship very much. Volunteers feel good knowing that they have helped an entrepreneur or someone in business overcome challenges. For more information, visit www.score.org.

Take Classes for a New Career: It's Never Too Late to Change Direction!

A number of resources within the community can assist you with a new career. A recent survey by New York University's School of Continuing and Professional Studies found that an overwhelming majority of college-educated professionals seek, above everything, greater fulfillment from their work and will pursue it in three or more different careers over their lifetimes. Thirty-four percent of the adult students surveyed said that career change was their primary motivation for enrolling in continuing education courses and programs, a big jump from 24 percent who said so in 2001.

Many community colleges and adult education programs at universities offer noncredit courses and certificates. They are a wonderful way to learn and meet others in a new field.

Over the years, I have referred many clients to certificate programs to pursue another line of work. Some people fear they might be the "oldest student" on campus. But as time passes, this scenario is becoming less likely because many are returning to school at an older age. Recently, I read about an eighty-year-old starting law school, and I have clients who have gone through the application process and one who decided to attend law school at an advanced age!

It's common to hear stories of how people changed their lives overnight, when it often takes years of false starts and trial and error. For example, I follow up regularly with my clients to see how they're doing years after our work together. I find that many didn't act on the information and ideas we put together until many years later. It takes time to integrate information about interests, skills, value systems, and personality style. For me, the satisfaction comes when people eventually make the needed changes and take the appropriate action to achieve their goals.

With a projected life span of an additional twenty years, does it really matter at what age you make the change? The crucial fact is that it doesn't matter when; it matters more that you do it at some point in your lifetime. So what if it takes three years to get a master's degree? Those three years will pass no matter what you do. But if you choose to pursue the degree, at the end of three years, you'll have it instead of merely wishing you did.

REAL-LIFE EXAMPLE: CAREER AND LIFE COACH

Sara has created a wonderful work/life balance for herself by leaving her full-time position in banking to work as a career and life coach three afternoons a week.

She'd worked very hard for many years in the banking industry, but she was always interested in becoming a career coach. She took the required courses and began working two nights a week to build up her private practice while she kept her banking job. After she left the bank as a full-time employee, she worked four days a week as a coach.

To maintain a balanced lifestyle, she has gradually cut back her working hours and stopped doing promotional work. She now relies solely on referrals. Over the past three years, she has been asked to work in an organization full-time or part-time, but she has declined these options because she likes being independent and making her own decisions. For the first time in her life, she also feels she has created balance because she's clear on what is important to her: staying in good physical shape, eating well, volunteering, and having fun.

Currently her greatest challenge is staying connected to the professional community, because working as an independent can become isolating. She keeps abreast of new developments in the field by reading and researching.

Sara feels she's been lucky to reach this phase in her career; however, I believe she created the circumstances for good things to happen. Her advice to others is never to give up on trying to achieve a satisfying career and not to get discouraged. She worked in many professions that were not satisfying before her work as a career coach; however, she continued to feel that you have to be committed to the belief that you will find the career that is right for you. According to her, you need to do what it takes to discover your interests, which may include going back to school. The key is to hold on to the belief that you can achieve fulfillment if you are willing to work for it.

REAL-LIFE EXAMPLES

The following are two examples of individuals who have achieved successful semi-retirement.

DENTAL ASSISTANT

A dental assistant I interviewed worked full time for twenty-eight years. Recently she started to work part-time, three days a week. Since her commute is an hour and a half each way, this change has made her life much easier. She works the latter half of the week—Wednesday, Thursday, and Friday. She still loves the structure that work provides, however, and after four days off, she feels rejuvenated and ready to return to the office.

ANTIQUES STORE OWNER

The man I interviewed worked in the garment business and owned a limousine company. His wife owned an antiques store, and when he retired from his other businesses, she asked him to join her. Since he had collected antiques for thirty years, he thought it was a great idea. The more he works in the business, the more he loves it. His passion turned into a part-time job instead of retirement. He works about twenty to thirty hours a week. He loves dealing with the customers and attending to the business needs, and he says that it gets him "out of the house." He doesn't like golf and feels he is too hyperactive for full retirement. He plans to work until he no longer can. He is young at heart, and his work helps him stay that way. To stay physically active, he walks three miles every day.

His enjoys the challenge of satisfying customers as well as taking care of day-to-day tasks: electrical work, going to the upholsterer, arranging deliveries, etc. Clearly, having this kind of purpose enhances his satisfaction with life. He also has the opportunity to work with his partner, whom he adores.

His advice to others is, if you want to be successful, you have to love what you do; work hard, and you'll be successful. While he knows people who love full retirement, he knows others, usually high-powered executives, who are very unhappy in retirement. He knows the right choice for him includes working part-time in a field he loves.

Resources for Seniors and Soon-to-Be-Seniors

- Contact your local and state government offices and Web sites for senior resources, including a list of senior centers in your area. Many government Web sites list jobs specific to older workers. State governments often have special divisions or committees on aging.
- www.2young2retire.com; resources to help make retirement as interesting as possible.
- www.40plus.org; helps managers, executives, and other professionals over age forty find new jobs or make career transitions
- AARP, www.aarp.org; among many other resources, lists the "Best Employers for People Over 50"
- Administration on Aging, www.aoa.gov
- www.civicventures.org; service-oriented opportunities for seniors
- U.S. Department of Labor's Employment and Training Program, www.doleta.gov, has a Senior Community Service Employment Program for those age fifty-five and older
- www.experienceworks.org; helps seniors get the training they need to find jobs
- National Council on Aging, www.ncoa.org; features, among other resources, the National Older Worker Partnership
- National Older Workers Career Center, www.nowcc.org; provides professional, technical, and administrative work opportunities

- www.peacecorps.gov; applicants include retirees
- www.retiredbrains.com; various job listings for retirees
- www.seniorcorps.gov; matches volunteers' skills and interests with opportunities in the community
- www.seniorjobbank.org; all types of jobs for those over age fifty
- www.seniorjobs.org
- www.seniorjournal.com
- www.seniorresource.com
- www.seniorserviceamerica.org; provides training and employment opportunities to older adults
- www.seniors4hire.org
- www.senior-site.com; resources for life after retirement
- www.thetransitionnetwork.org; an organization for women at or approaching retirement
- www.yourencore.com; recruits experienced professionals, primarily scientists, engineers, and product developers

CHAPTER 9

Perfect for Those Seeking a Better Lifestyle

"Living in balance and purity
is the highest good for you and the earth."
—Dr. Deepak Chopra

In many ways, this entire book is about achieving a work/life balance. We've discussed how many parents, caregivers, aging baby boomers, and seniors need and want to find a balance between earning money and living the life they want to live. But you don't have to be nearing retirement or taking care of a family to appreciate a reduced work schedule. Maybe you just want time for yourself—to explore the world, to explore your art or passions, or simply to live a less hectic life.

We are from such a work-oriented, work-ethic culture that single or married-without-children, young or middle-aged adults are often made to feel guilty if they're not working forty-plus hours a week. We need a new paradigm for living. Sure, we want to be complete, active, productive human beings. I'm not advocating becoming a slacker or a couch potato. I am suggesting, however, that we reevaluate what living a full, productive life means.

If it means slaving away full-time at a job you hate while ignoring aspects of your one and only life that could make living worthwhile, *then* I say it's time for a change. You could figure out how to work thirty hours a week or less and find time to volunteer, learn to play an instrument or speak a foreign language, or simply take better care of your physical, emotional, intellectual, and spiritual self.

The desire to achieve a more suitable work/life balance for yourself is an excellent reason for going part-time. It may improve your sanity and your outlook, and if you've developed unhealthy workaholic habits—overeating, drinking, and drug taking (over-the-counter or otherwise)—you very well might save your life.

I have seen an influx of people in my private practice who seem willing to give up money to find work that is less demanding and more fulfilling. Many are beginning to see that you can't buy back the hours lost to an obsessive work style. How much money are they willing to give up? This is a personal question. We need to understand our priorities to figure out how much is enough.

Sound Familiar?

A young woman who came to the United States from China at the age of eighteen was able to observe the way overwork can slowly yet surely degrade our health and lifestyle. When Grace first came to this country two years ago, she made friends with people working in the financial industry. She found them to be very smart and efficient individuals who had graduated from Ivy League schools. Initially, she was very impressed with their lives. However, as time passed, she gradually began to notice that they complained quite often about their heavy workload and the toll it took on them.

One friend of hers, an equity trader on Wall Street, described his life this way: He was full of energy and ready for action on Monday. The overexcitement, however, left him stressed and depressed by Tuesday and overwhelmed by the amount of work that had already piled up on his desk. By Wednesday, he'd have trouble breathing and was fantasizing about the weekend. By Thursday, he felt there was just no way to survive without having two expensive coffees to get him through the day. By Friday, he was past the point of caring. All he wanted to do was to finish and get out by 5:00 pm to start living his "real" two-day life over the weekend.

The question is: How many years will these people (or you, if the shoe fits) be able to withstand this lifestyle?

Generation X

Many studies have shown that Generation Xers (those born between 1965 and 1980, or the after-baby boomers) have a greater need and desire for work/life balance than do other generations. Work is not the most important thing to them; they value their personal time. It's really a benefit for companies to offer work/life incentives to their Generation X employees.

According to Charlotte and Laura Shelton, authors of *The Next Revolution: What Gen X Women Want at Work and How Their Boomer Bosses Can Help Them Get It*:

- 61 percent of Gen X women said they'd leave their job for one that was more flexible;
- 52 percent said they would go elsewhere to work fewer hours; and
- 51 percent said they'd quit if another employer offered them the chance to telecommute.

A Balanced Life Makes You a More Successful and Attractive Person

When you maintain your physical, emotional, mental, and spiritual well-being, you put yourself in the best position for success in your professional and private life. When you reduce your work hours, you gain in the following areas:

- Time—It's good to have at least one hour each day just for you.
- Space—It's good to have room to think and be without pressure or obligation.

- Energy and vitality—You need to have enough oomph to get through the day, and you need enough time to rest well at night.
- Momentum—You need strength to keep going and growing.
- Power—You gain the ability to act with vigor.

Signs that Your Life Is Out of Balance

There are some sure-fire signs that your life is out of balance.

DIET

Lack of time encourages many to eat on the run, which unfortunately results in eating foods that are high in fat and calories. When you're always in a rush, you sometimes forget to eat, causing blood sugar to vary greatly. I've had clients who were very irritated, easy to anger, and stressed out all the time because of their poor eating habits. During the day they rarely ate lunch, so later in the day they binged on poor food choices. When they began to realize that their food intake contributed to their bad mood and low energy level, they made some changes. One individual in particular made a conscious effort to keep and eat healthy snacks at her desk. A co-worker who had typically irked her and caused her distress began to bother her less. She is convinced that paying attention to her diet has helped. In addition, working long hours and eating a later dinner contributes to weight problems and irritability.

This is not a minor issue. Diet, or rather a poor diet, is associated with a host of ills. Taking care of yourself is a major reason to consider part-time work.

EXERCISE

Unfortunately, when people get too busy, exercise is one of the first things to go. If you don't have any time in your life for physical activity, it's time to reevaluate your schedule and reorganize your priorities.

We all know by now the many benefits of exercise. When

you free up your schedule, you have more time to go to the gym, take an exercise class, run, walk, or ride a bike. It doesn't matter what you choose, just that you are active for part of the day.

Everyone I interviewed agreed that a part-time schedule gives them more time to exercise. Unfortunately, many people feel the pressure to exercise only after getting a poor report from the doctor or when facing a medical problem. They react instead of being proactive.

SPIRITUALITY

For many, their spiritual needs are being sapped. Some individuals would like to become more involved in religious organizations and in their communities, but they do not have the time. All of their resources are devoted to their work and other personal needs. When my clients do the exercise in the following section, many are disappointed and frustrated to see how many of the boxes they leave blank. Unfortunately, spirituality is often one of the most neglected areas in the overworked person's life.

FUN

Raise your hand if you're fun-deprived. You're not alone. Fun and laughter are key elements of a happy and successful life, but like everything else, they take time and effort. Laughter has been known to help many through a difficult time, and a good laugh has been associated with improving health and reducing stress. There are even classes and conferences devoted to the value of laughter.

When I say, "fun," I don't just mean wild, raucous times. You should also have time in your life for hobbies or simply to relax, read a book, or listen to music.

Find the Gaps in Your Life

To help people get a clear idea of where they're spending their energy and what they're missing, I ask many of my clients to complete the following exercise, which was given to me many years ago by a fellow coach: What activities do you pursue in the following areas of your life? List a regular activity or activities under each category.

Health/Well-Being   Relationship/Family

Career/Business   Pleasure/Recreation

Money/Finances   Spiritual/Religious

Learning/Personal   Other

It's very revealing and startling to people when many of the boxes are empty, and they realize they need to make a change to attain a more fulfilling life. They often realize that they work too much.

Where to Start

Everyone talks about balancing work and personal lives, but how do we really do it, considering all of our roles and responsibilities? Begin by asking yourself: "How can I make my work as well as my personal life more meaningful?"

Balance is a life full of what is important to you. To attain harmony, we need to think about the things that are most important to us in our personal and professional lives and pursue those activities first. This can raise hard questions, but making a conscious choice about our priorities helps us to achieve greater satisfaction.

I believe in taking small steps to achieve success. Change doesn't happen overnight nor should it. Furthermore, I recommend that my clients take one action a day toward their goals, especially their long-term goal. Strength builds on strength. Get moving. Build momentum. Steady effort counts for more than you'd imagine. Each action builds on itself. Every step along the way matters. For example, I always knew that I wanted to start my own career counseling business. While I was working as a consultant, this seemed like an overwhelming long-term task and goal. I decided, therefore, to take one action a day toward starting a career counseling business, and it worked.

Psychological Readiness

We all need to establish strategic and psychological readiness. Psychological readiness includes recognizing your obstacles and barriers. Ask yourself what's holding you back, what's blocking you? It might be real or imagined. Checking out the reality of your fears with a trusted adviser can be very helpful.

Many of us fear change, and we need to understand that fear before we take action. You can begin to understand your fears by talking with others and acquiring as much information as possible about your undertaking. Talking your fears through with an objective professional is ideal. The more you embrace and understand your perceived obstacles, the better able you are to assess the situation and make the best decision for yourself (see chapter 3 for more information on learning to take risks and face change and on finding a professional career and life coach).

Sometimes you merely need to recharge your batteries. I have recommended to clients in need of a change that they take on a temporary assignment, even in something not seen as a potential career opportunity. For example, if you work behind a desk and are unhappy with the lack of human contact, try working in a customer service capacity. Moves like this can revive those who have become stuck in a rut.

It make take some extra effort initially, but you can do these "try-out" experiences while maintaining your full-time position just to get a taste of what a different position would be like.

Before figuring out what's next, the key is to begin to feel better and more like yourself. A bad work situation can wear you down in a very destructive way. You need to begin to repair the damage before moving on. Try to make improvements in at least one area in your life—something that gets you on the right track to being you.

Strategies to Balance Work with the Rest of Your Life

PRIORITIZE

Do what's most important first. To figure out what is most important to you, you need to recognize that priorities and values change over time, and you should constantly readjust your list.

Sometimes it's easier to ask yourself what you love to do with your time. If you're a parent, is it the ability to stay home with your child and watch him or her throughout daily routines? Is it more important to take extended business trips to help in career promotion? Is it the security of a steady stream of income? Is it the power of your old position? The professional status you have achieved? The freedom to leave home every day? There are no right or wrong answers to these questions; however, it's important to know that your answer will change as your life changes.

Ideally, you want the time and effort you spend on activities to be in sync with your values, and you want your values to guide your decisions. Begin this process by identifying what is most significant to you, then budget your time and choices accordingly.

It's often easier to look at your values as if you were budgeting your money. Where would you want to spend your money? Prioritize the following according to their importance to you:

- success in your career
- friendships with others
- high-status job
- entrepreneurship
- self-confidence
- peace of mind
- healthy lifestyle
- volunteer/philanthropic activities
- financial security
- autonomy
- creativity
- adventure
- family time

SET GOALS

Exploring your present value system, skills, and interests is an excellent way to begin the process of determining the most suitable personal and professional goals. I recommend that my clients set three-month goals. Each goal requires two specific action steps (see chapter 3 for extensive information on determining values, interests, and skills sets and for the "Goal Sheet" exercise).

TIME MANAGEMENT

Time management is key to maintaining work/life balance. First, time management is about learning how to prioritize. Second, it's about learning how to say no. We all have our personal boundaries and need to honor them by acknowledging what we can and cannot take on. We set boundaries to protect ourselves from other peoples' insensitive or irresponsible behavior. A boundary is basically a no.

It's very helpful to get into the habit of underpromising and overdelivering. Many people promise themselves and others too much. Experience has shown that most people are more comfortable when they promise less and accomplish more. Trying to keep up with too many promises depletes one of energy.

Parents Aren't the Only Ones Who Need Time and Balance

Childless workers and managers often find themselves pitching in when others are out for maternity leave or taking care of their children. It's only natural that there would be some resentment. I hear it from my clients who are placed in that position. There should be more allowances for their circumstances as well. These people feel others at work are less willing to help them when they ask for time off for personal obligations.

If you find yourself in this category, you need to be proactive and make certain that your personal needs rank as high as those with children or others with care-giving responsibilities. If you feel burdened because others take time off for personal reasons much more than you do, perhaps you can schedule an appointment with your manager to discuss this and find alternatives.

According to E. Michelle Bohreer, chairman of the litigation and employment group of the Boyar and Miller Law Firm, in Houston, in 2005, "A flextime policy should be applied consistently and fairly across the company whether you are married or have children . . . . That means your decision to use the flex policy to take salsa lessons should be weighted equally with another's decision to pick up the children after school" ("The Childless Need Weekends, Too" by Cheryl Dahle, *New York Times*).

The Center for WorkLife Law at the University of California, Hastings College of the Law, provides "sociological and legal perspectives" on the issue of childless workers who think they don't get the benefits that those with children do (http://www.uchastings.edu/?pid = 3633).

Money Matters

Before many people feel the freedom to take on part-time work, they need to feel financially secure. The scariest part of going part-time is often the financial sacrifice. Interestingly enough, when you begin to explore this with people, they start to realize that they are spending a lot of money on "things" to compensate for the strain and unhappiness of working long hours at jobs they don't like or that cause them stress.

I ask many of my clients to prepare a budget to get a sense where their money goes. Inevitably, many of the expenses are for "creature comforts." When they begin to analyze their life and work and imagine themselves happy, they realize they usually don't need as much money. (See chapter 2 for information and exercises to help you determine your financial readiness for a reduced-hour career.)

REAL-LIFE EXAMPLE

I have a wonderful example to demonstrate this. Kim, a high-powered lawyer who was on track to become a partner, came to see me. She was impeccably dressed. During our first session she cried the entire time, telling me how unhappy she was. The job did not draw on her strengths and interests; however, she was doing very well and was on partner track, in spite of her unhappiness. She was a very bright and articulate woman who appeared to be happier on the surface than she was.

As we got to know one another, she told me she spent *all* her free time (which was not a lot) shopping. Her wardrobe exemplified this. Shopping became a sabotaging and addictive habit to ameliorate her sadness and frustration with her work.

During subsequent sessions, we explored her fears and the obstacles to her leaving her current position. One of her greatest fears was that she would not have the income to spend on clothing and dining out. It was only when she realized why she was spending the money (to hide her pain) that she was able to see she didn't actually enjoy how she was spending her money.

We explored her interests, skills, values, and personal preferences, and she realized that her job was not well suited to her, and she chose to pursue teaching law abroad. During our last session before she left to go abroad, she came to my office beaming, dressed very casually in jeans.

Location, Location, Location

One factor that plays an important role in both your satisfaction with your personal life and the amount of money you need to achieve your goals in life is where you live. Unfortunately, many people run themselves ragged on the never-ending work treadmill so they can afford to live in an area that—get this— they don't want to live in to begin with! They put up with traffic, outrageous real estate prices, and incredible costs of living— and for what? So they can go to a job they dislike and work at it forty-plus hours a week?

I suggest to my clients that they think seriously about where they live and, if possible, consider relocating to a less expensive area. One word of caution, however. Moving is a major life stressor, so you need to consider it very carefully. Where you live affects the quality of your life, perhaps more than any other factor. Give it serious thought, and you might find you'll be able to live on less and pursue your dreams.

Questions to Ponder While Trying to Determine Your Dream Location

What are your fears about moving? What would you be giving up? If the problem is leaving relatives behind—aging parents or siblings—can you maintain your relationship through frequent visits?

- What would you gain? What are you trying to achieve by moving?
- What are your key priorities in a new home, for example,

climate, medical facilities nearby, close to family, access to hobbies?

- What age people do you primarily want in your community, that is, families with young children, singles, seniors, a variety?
- What are your environmental preferences? Close to an ocean, a lake, a river, mountains? Do you prefer city, small-town, or country living?
- Apartment, condo, townhouse, or single-family home? Lease or rent? How much can you afford each month? How many bedrooms or square feet do you need and want? How much land can you enjoy before it becomes a burden?
- What are your favorite and least favorite weather patterns?
- When do you want to move? When can you move?
- How much money do you have set aside for moving costs and initial costs for your new home? Perhaps you need to consult with a financial adviser and/or banker.
- What do you consider the ideal location? In other words, what place have you always dreamed of or fantasized about? Make a list of pros and cons. What do you like about the place? What do you dislike? What kind of work could you do there?

REAL-LIFE EXAMPLE: RELOCATION

Alex, a past client of mine, lived in New York and worked in a bank. Although she had friends and family close by, Alex loved California. All her education and training had prepared her for the job in New York, but she loved the outdoors and the more casual life California offered. She did a lot of research on places where she could live in California. She also began subscribing to local California papers to get a feel for the economy, cultures, housing market, etc. After discussing the pros and cons, she took an extended trip there, had several job interviews, and spent time with friends and acquaintances. Alex ended up making the move. The last time I spoke with her she was very happy.

Tips for Relocating

DON'T MAKE A HASTY DECISION

After sorting out the pros and cons, give yourself a "timeout" before making the final decision. We often react to our present circumstances in a panic mode rather than fully understanding the ramifications of our decisions. When I work with clients considering relocation, I always recommend that they spend adequate time and devote adequate thought before making the final decision.

CHECK YOUR CREDIT RATING

It's helpful to know your credit rating. There are three major credit bureaus: Equifax, Experian, and TransUnion. According to the Federal Trade Commission, "After September 1, 2005, U.S. consumers will be eligible to request a free report. Annualcreditreport.com is the only authorized source for consumers to access their credit reports online for free."

Consumers may also request a free credit report by calling, toll-free, 877-322-8228. For more information on free reports or how to dispute errors, visit the Federal Trade Commission's Web site at www.ftc.gov/credit. If you want to explore credit counseling, visit the National Foundation for Credit Counseling (www.nfcc.org) for information and a list of members.

CLEAN OUT YOUR CLOSETS

Even before you make the final decision to move, start preparing. You may actually make a better decision with less clutter around. Your mind will be clearer without unnecessary items to distract you. Start by discarding one item each day. Before you know it, you'll feel less overwhelmed, and you'll begin to see the results of your efforts.

Relocation Resources

- www.bestplaces.net; evaluates cities based on cost of living, crime rates, climate, school statistics, etc.

- Chamber of Commerce, uschamberofcommerce.com or www.chamberofcommerce.com; go to the appropriate chamber of commerce to find a wealth of information on a location and click on links to specific areas
- www.cityrating.com; provides information on metropolitan areas
- www.citysearch.com
- www.epodunk.com; features detailed profiles of more than 46,000 places in the United States
- www.findyourspot.com; includes an online quiz to help you find places that match your lifestyle interests
- Government Web sites; state and local government Web sites are great places to start investigating a given area. Most have valuable information on schools, hospitals, population, cost of living, etc. Check out governmentguide.com for links. The Small Business Association, www.sba.gov, has lists of helpful local offices if you plan to start or buy a business.
- www.homefair.com; lots of information on relocating, including salary and moving calculators
- Internet browsers and search engines—AOL, Yahoo, Google, etc.—have frontpage links to their real estate sites that allow you to research neighborhoods, housing, shopping, etc. Or go to a search engine such as www.google.com and type in the name of the town and state or county and state, along with the word, "relocate."
- www.kidfriendlycities.org
- Magazines; many feature special issues on "best places to live" based on the interests of their readers. For example, *Outside* magazine listed "best towns" based on the following criteria: commitment to open space, intelligent answers to traffic and congestion, good community energy, lots of fun/outdoor activities, nice lush design, environmentally friendly surroundings, good healthy produce, and a vibrant job market.
- www.newspaperlinks.com

- www.newspapers.com
- www.money.cnn.com/best/bplive; annual best places to live list
- www.realestatejournal.com; *Wall Street Journal*'s guide to property
- www.realtor.com; real estate listings and information, including relocation resources
- www.relocationcentral.com; an apartment finder
- www.ruralize.com Features links to websites on country living and promote the outstanding book *How to Find Your Country Home*, by Gene Gerue.
- www.theschoolreport.com

Real-Life Examples

AN INVESTMENT BANKER RE-CREATES HIMSELF

The smartest people I know have decided to take a timeout at some point in their career to reassess their goals and values. A client of mine, who had a law degree from one of the top universities in the country, had worked at an investment bank in New York for many years. Others perceived him as doing a wonderful job, but he was miserable inside. His weight had skyrocketed, his health had begun to deteriorate, and he had virtually no personal life. It was one of the most difficult decisions of his life to leave the investment bank, but he did and he's never looked back.

His first impulse was to take time off to figure out what to do next. He went abroad for a while and immersed himself in another culture and language to recharge. When he returned from his time abroad, he contacted me and we began to work together to determine a career and life plan. Because he's an incredibly thorough and intelligent man, he based his decision on his interests, skills, values, needs, and personality style.

He was not originally from New York and decided to return to an area of the country closer to his roots. His new role included being a real estate entrepreneur, which was more in line with his strengths and preferences. He worked fewer hours than he had as an investment banker (cutting down to forty hours a week seemed like part-time to him). At heart, he was an outdoors man, and the last time I spoke with him, he was involved in triathlons and felt physically well. A change of career and lifestyle worked for him, and it can work for you when you take time to figure out what is best for you.

Remember, your priorities and values vary over time, and you need to adjust accordingly. It takes courage and confidence, but it can be done.

ADJUNCT PROFESSOR/ART COLLECTOR

Mindy was a full-time professor for twenty-seven years. For ten of those years she commuted from Massachusetts to New York City on the weekends because her husband lived and worked in New York. While she was on sabbatical, she decided to stay in New York permanently. She liked her job, but she was sick of spending so much time in the car. She also had no time for herself. Now she's teaching one class in New York City and collecting American art, a passion she's had throughout the years.

She's enjoying the freedom and flexibility of not being confined to a strict schedule. The challenge is that she doesn't feel connected to any institution and doesn't have a single mission. This is not unusual. After living and working with such an intense schedule for many years, a person can feel lost when it comes to making a lifestyle change. That doesn't mean you shouldn't make a change, just be prepared for and aware of the challenges of transition.

LIVING HER VALUES IN TERMS OF BOTH WORK AND TIME

A woman I interviewed moved to a small community with her husband and five-year-old daughter. She chose a small community because she wanted to live out her lifestyle preferences, which included becoming involved in the community and working to improve the environment.

She believes so passionately about maintaining a simple life that at one time she taught a class, entitled "Simplify and Enrich Your Life." The message she wanted to communicate is that life is to be spent on your passions rather than on accumulating unnecessary "stuff." She is not a huge consumer, and she educates people to become more aware of what they actually need.

To maintain a balanced personal life, she and her husband agreed that each would work five years and then switch off, so their daughter would always have a parent at home. Their daughter was homeschooled, and their highest priority was spending as much time as possible with her while she was growing up.

To live the life they wanted, they rearranged their finances, paying careful attention to their expenses. She thinks so many people go to work, only to have to spend their hard-earned dollars on clothes, transportation, and day care. She believes they could live on a lot less and be home with their children more if they took the time to evaluate their priorities. Perhaps, many more people can make going part-time affordable if they consider switching roles intermittently with their partner.

According to this woman, to have balance you need time to reflect. Essentially, her goal is to live according to her value system. When this is established, she is able to make conscious, intentional choices.

Over the years, her work schedule increased. Now that her daughter is grown up, she works full-time, but she and her partner exemplify how people can adjust and modify their needs and values at specific times in their lives.

At this point in her career, she is evaluating environmental programs in terms of sustainability, which she finds tremendously gratifying. Once again, she finds herself evaluating and assessing—a key component in making good choices.

Web Resources

- Take Back Your Time, www.simpleliving.net/timeday; this

organization defines itself as a "major initiative to challenge the epidemic of overwork, over-scheduling and time famine that now threatens our health, our families and relationships, our communities and our environment." Extensive links and resource information

- http://getmoredone.com/tips.html; insightful tips on how to plan your day, simplify life, reduce stress, stop procrastinating, etc.
- http://imt.net/ ~ randolfi/StressLinks.html; stress management and emotional wellness links
- www.maximumbalance.com
- http://mindtools.com/smpage.html; provides information and programs that help you deal with work-related stress
- The American Institute of Stress, http://www.stress.org/; learn to understand and cope with stress
- www.worklifebalance.com; provides Web-based training and support programs such as stress management and time management to help people achieve their goals and enjoy life

Book Resources

- *The Art of the Possible*, Alexandra Stoddard, 1996.
- *Burnout: How to Beat the High Cost of Success*, Dr. Herbert J. Freudenberger, 1980.
- *Calling: Finding and Following an Authentic Life*, Gregg Levoy, 1998.
- *Chop Wood, Carry Water: A Guide to Finding Spiritual Fulfillment in Everday Life*, editors of *New Age Journal*, 1984.
- *Do What You Love: The Money Will Follow*, Marsha Sinetar, 1989.
- *Flow: The Psychology of Optimal Experience*, Mihaly Csikszentmihalyi, 1991.
- *Get a Life Without Sacrificing Your Career*, Dianna Booher, 1996.

- *Getting Organized*, Stephanie Winston, 1991.
- *I Could Do Anything If I Only Knew What*, Barbara Sher, 1995.
- *If You Haven't Got the Time to Do It Right, When Will You Find the Time to Do It Over?* Jeffrey J. Mayer, 1991.
- *I'll Work for Free*, Bob Weinstein, 1994.
- *Just Enough: Tools for Creating Success in Your Work and Life*, Laura Nash and Howard Stevenson, 2005.
- *Living Happily Ever After*, Marsha Sinetar, 1990.
- *Making a Living Without a Job: Winning Ways for Creating the Work You Love*, Barbara Winter, 1993.
- *The Next Revolution: What Gen X Women Want at Work and How Their Boomer Bosses Can Help Them Get It*, Charlotte Shelton and Laura Shelton, 2005.
- *Organizing from the Inside Out*, Julie Morgenstern, 1998.
- *Overwhelmed: Coping with Life's Ups and Downs*, Nancy Schlossberg, 1999.
- *The Power of Purpose*, Richard Leider, 1997.
- *Repacking Your Bags: Lighten Your Load for the Rest of Your Life*, Richard Leider and David Shapiro, 2002.
- *Simplify Your Life: 100 Ways to Slow Down and Enjoy the Things That Really Matter*, Elaine St. James, 1994.
- *Sometimes Enough Is Enough*, Marsha Sinetar, 2000.
- *Take Time for Your Life*, Cheryl Richardson, reprint, 1999.
- *To Build the Life You Want, Create the Work You Love*, Marsha Sinetar, 1995.
- *You Don't Have to Go Home from Work Exhausted*, A. McGee-Cooper, 1992.

CHAPTER 10

Job Search Overview: Your Personal Pitch, Resumes, Cover Letters, and Interviews

Ready, Set, Go!

Y ou've read a lot, now it's time to get into action. In this chapter, I show you how to create a personal pitch, prepare your resume and cover letter, and prepare for employment interviews. Don't let this part of the process overwhelm you; take it one step at a time. Remember, strength builds on strength.

Informal Networking

I discussed the value of networking in chapter 6, but let's go over some key concepts again. Meeting with informal contacts will help you learn more about your industry and individual job prospects. Networking can also help you clarify and strengthen your career plans before you begin your job interviews.

Networking meetings should be informal. Try to keep them simple and low key. Before contacting someone by phone or email, make sure you have a definite link or referral to the person and a reason for calling. You can then set up an appointment at a time and place convenient to the contact. If the contact is too busy, ask if you can pick his or her brain over the phone.

The discussion should be purely informational and exploratory. That way neither of you will feel the pressures and constraints of an actual employment interview. Lunch or after-work meetings are recommended.

If you're fortunate enough to meet a contact who works in an organization in which you are interested, this is an ideal opportunity to find out specifics about the position and the company. This type of networking gives you a chance to get the inside information you could never get in a job interview, so take advantage of it. Preparation and follow-up greatly increase the value of these meetings. Take good notes; they will be useful in the future. Business dress is most appropriate for these meetings, but, again, don't try to turn the situation into a job interview. The person with whom you are meeting may resent this. After the meeting, write a thank-you letter to the person you visited.

Personal Pitch

Let's say you meet a recruiter at a career fair or are introduced to a key player in your chosen field. You need to be able to tell that person who you are, what your experience is, and what you're looking for, all in a short amount of time. Don't try to cover everything, only the pertinent information. Today most people are extremely busy and have short attention spans, so you need to create a succinct way to introduce yourself in less than a minute. Perfecting a personal pitch is difficult, but not impossible.

This is your opportunity to make a positive impression. Think about what you want to say and practice it with a trusted friend or professional. You want to sound natural and not rehearsed. The most helpful framework is: Make your message clear.

- Introduction. Example: "Hello, I'm Sue Jones. I've been in sales and marketing for a number of years. I'm currently preparing to reenter the workplace after taking time off to raise my children. Any advice you could give me would be greatly appreciated." At this point, you've given the person a snapshot of where you fit in—sales and marketing—and an idea of what you're looking for. Then move on to:

- Your general background. This is the guts of the pitch. In this portion of your pitch, expand on your most valued skills in ways that show you would be a benefit to an organization or employer. Be enthusiastic and involve the listener. You might want to mention a few related accomplishments as well as key personality traits that make you successful. Example: "I've worked in the sales and marketing division of the pharmaceutical industry for ten years, where I was responsible for more than eighty accounts. During that time, the efficiency of my division increased by 10 percent. I pride myself on being a team player and a hard worker, and I value that in an employer as well."

- Ending. Ask for any suggestions or observations the person may have, and if you could meet him or her for lunch or coffee for further general discussion. Example: "I know you have a lot of experience in the industry, and I'd appreciate any feedback or ideas you may have. Is it possible to meet or speak again in the near future?" Make sure you thank the person for his or her time at the end of the conversation.

Your goal is to become skilled at communicating your pitch and using it whenever possible. You'll have to adapt it for the situation. You never know where a potential job may come from; you could get a lead at a social function, community event, professional meeting, or simply through the course of everyday life. If you run into someone in one of these settings, and a conversation starts, you can rely on your personal pitch, which you've perfected, to ensure that you cover the important points.

The two most neglected words are "thank you." Everyone appreciates being thanked. If managers, bosses, and supervisors remembered this, there would be many more happy employees in the workplace. In addition to saying thanks after any meeting or interview, send a thank-you note. You may send an email, a typed snail mail letter, or a handwritten note. I know candidates who believe a handwritten note helped them get a job offer. A "thank you" is also appreciated if someone went out of his or her way to make an introduction for you. If it's done in a sincere way, I don't believe you can say thank you enough.

Brainstorming Your Resume

Like any good marketing campaign—and that is precisely what a job search is—you need to define the product—a combination of your accomplishments, motivated skills, values, interests, personality style, and priorities.

To showcase your product (you), you need to prepare a resume. The first step is to identify and define your work and accomplishments. All of us accomplish things every day, but many of us take our accomplishments for granted. Therefore, you need to take stock of them and list them so you can refer to them as needed. When you give specific examples, you demonstrate your abilities better. Think of things that have given you satisfaction, that you performed well, and that you felt good about. In an accomplishment statement, you want to explain what you did, how you did it, and what the result was. Think of examples in your life where you developed, initiated, created, prepared, were involved in, implemented, organized, assisted, designed, and/or changed something. These are true accomplishments.

Types of Resumes

A resume mentions your skills and accomplishments in a positive way. Some people refer to it as your marketing tool. There are two main types of resumes.

The *chronological resume* focuses on your employment history (list in reverse order with the most recent dates first). It is more common, and many people prefer it.

The *functional resume* groups accomplishments and skills under separate categories—sales, marketing, management, planning, etc. This may be more appropriate for those who are initiating a major career change or who have had many short-term jobs. This can be effective when you want to sell your skills to a different industry or for a different position. It can be extremely helpful when searching for a different career goal since you can erase the specifics of your experience and try to emphasize your transferable skills.

Remember, the purpose of a resume is to get an interview. It must be interesting and intriguing enough to accomplish this. Your resume can be general, and you can tailor your cover letter to each specific situation.

Typically, your resume should not be more than two pages; try hard to keep it to one. It should also be easy to read with bullets and space between sections. You need to choose carefully which accomplishments are most pertinent to your new situation (see the sample resumes at the end of this chapter). Use action words to describe your experience and accomplishments.

Action Words for Effective Resumes

A	Audited	Coauthored
Accomplished	Authored	Collaborated
Achieved		Collated
Acted	**B**	Collected
Administered	Began	Communicated
Advised	Booked	Compared
Allocated	Broadened	Compiled
Analyzed	Budgeted	Completed
Applied		Composed
Appraised	**C**	Computed
Appreciated	Calculated	Conceived
Arbitrated	Catalogued	Condensed
Arranged	Changed	Conducted
Assembled	Charted	Confronted
Assessed	Classified	Constructed
Assisted	Coached	Contacted

Contracted
Controlled
Cooked
Coordinated
Counseled
Created

D
Decided
Decorated
Defined
Delegated
Delivered
Demonstrated
Described
Designed
Determined
Developed
Devised
Directed
Displayed
Distributed
Drafted

E
Earned
Educated
Effected
Elicited
Eliminated
Encouraged
Enforced
Enlisted
Entertained
Escorted
Established
Evaluated
Exhibited
Expanded
Explained
Exported

F
Facilitated
Fashioned
Figured
Filed
Fixed
Followed
Formulated
Funded

G
Gathered
Generated
Graphed
Guarded
Guided

H
Handled
Headed
Helped
Hired

I
Identified
Illustrated
Implemented
Imported
Improved
Increased
Indicated
Influenced
Initiated
Inquired
Inspected
Installed
Instituted
Interviewed
Introduced
Invented
Isolated
Itemized

J
Joined

K
Kept

L
Labeled
Landscaped
Layout
Learned
Led
Listed
Listened
Located

M
Maintained
Managed
Mapped
Matched
Measured
Memorized
Modeled
Modified
Molded
Monitored
Motivated

N
Navigated
Negotiated

O
Observed
Obtained
Operated
Ordered
Organized
Originated
Outlined

Overhauled
Oversaw

P
Painted
Participated
Persuaded
Photographed
Planned
Played
Prepared
Preserved
Prevented
Printed
Processed
Produced
Programmed
Promoted
Proposed
Protected
Provided

Q
Qualified
Questioned

R
Raised
Read
Received
Recognized
Recommended
Reconstructed

Recorded
Recruited
Rectified
Reduced
Reestablished
Reinforced
Reorganized
Repaired
Replaced
Reported
Represented
Researched
Reshaped
Responded
Retrieved
Revamped
Reviewed
Revised
Rewrote

S
Saved
Scheduled
Searched
Selected
Served
Setup
Simplified
Sketched
Sold
Solved
Spoke
Started

Streamlined
Strengthened
Structured
Studied

T
Tabulated
Taught
Tested
Took care of
Traced
Trained
Transcribed
Transferred
Translated
Treated
Tutored
Typed

U
Unified
Updated
Used

V
Verified
Visualized

W
Waited on
Widened
Worked

Parts of a Resume

- *Heading*: Include your name, address, telephone number, email address and website if you have one. If your resume is longer than one page, include your name on the second page as well, just in case the pages get separated.

- *Objective*: This is optional. One benefit of including an objective is that it tells the reader exactly what you're looking for. To avoid being too limiting, you may state your objective in broad terms. Another technique is to have two or more resumes with different objectives.
  Sample objectives:

  - To obtain a part-time nursing position in a hospital setting
  - To obtain a part-time accounting position in a major accounting firm

- *Summary*: Also optional, this briefly describes your background and experience. It may include key strengths, years of experience, types of organizations you worked for, or specific sales numbers, if pertinent.
  Sample summary statements:

  - Twelve years' experience as a financial professional with strong technical, computer, and accounting skills and a strong track record of motivating others.
  - An experienced sales professional responsible for more than $3 million in consumer sales.

- *Experience*: This is the nuts and bolts of your resume. Pay most attention to this section. For paid employment, it's best to label this "professional experience," "experience," "career background," or "employment history."

  - In the *chronological resume*, the experience section usually follows the objective and summary sections. Provide the name and location of the firm, your title, and your responsibilities. If the name of the company is unfamiliar to many, you may choose to explain the nature, size, or scope of the company or division. For dates, use years only. The only exception to this is if you are a student or recent graduate with limited experience. Try to avoid gaps if possible. The best language includes action words and short, results-oriented statements. For your most recent experience, select your most impressive accomplishments and bullet (indent) them. Don't use too many words or list too many accomplishments. You will be able to address additional accomplishments in the interview. Your earlier experience needs less explanation.

■ For the *functional resume*, you may title the section "key accomplishments" and mention three areas of accomplishment and bullet a few in each section. In a functional resume, you then list the dates and places you worked on the bottom of the resume (see the sample functional resume at the end of this chapter).

● *Education*: This is the next section in both types of resumes. Usually this appears below the "experience" section. However, if you're a recent graduate or a student and you have little paid experience, you may choose to list your education at the top of the resume. In this section, include not only formal education but additional training, professional certification, licenses, internships, honors, or scholarships as well.

● *Miscellaneous*: Many people have additional information to include such as military experience, languages, special skills, and organizational memberships. You may call this section "professional affiliations," "professional development," "other work experience," "special skills," "volunteer experience," "awards," and "community service."

Designing a Resume

The design of your resume is key. If you're mailing a hard copy of a resume, make sure it's on good-quality white paper; don't use colored paper or "cute" graphics. Make sure to leave enough white space. Use single spaces within paragraphs and double spaces between block-style paragraphs.

Since many people email resumes, make sure your electronic resumes are attachment-ready. I recommend that you send a test run to someone you know before sending your resume out to make sure it's presentable and easily read. Two sites that offer good information on how to prepare your resume files so that they may be easily emailed and posted are:

- Quintessential Careers, www.quintcareers.com
- The Riley Guide, www.rileyguide.com

Before you hit the send button on the computer or put your resume in the mail, make sure you like it. Does it look professional? Is the length appropriate? Is it action-oriented? Does it highlight your accomplishments? Is *every* single word spelled correctly? Are there any grammatical mistakes? Don't trust spell and grammar check alone; read it carefully. Have someone else proofread it as well.

Cover Letter

A cover letter usually accompanies your resume. There are two types of cover letters: a cover letter responding to a posted position and a cold-call cover letter in which you are investigating the possibility of a position within a targeted organization. In the second type of cover letter, you request a meeting, even if the company doesn't have a position. It is especially appropriate to send a targeted mailing if you're looking for a part-time position, and you know of a company that has work/life balance or family-friendly policies.

Address the letter to a specific person if a name is available on a posted position. For a targeted mailing, visit the organization's Web site or call the company to get the correct contact information; make sure you spell the contact's name correctly. Try to address the letter to the person who has the power to hire you, but follow the instructions in the job posting.

Here's the general formula for writing a cover letter:

First paragraph: Opening. If you're applying for a posted position, mention the exact position and why you are applying for it. Example: "I am applying for the advertised position of recreation coordinator. I believe my ten years' experience organizing after-school activities for the Kentucky public school system makes me well suited to the position." For a targeted mailing, enthusiastically express your interest in the organization.

Second paragraph: List your accomplishments. Stick to those that closely match the posted position. For a targeted mailing, list accomplishments you feel would be of value to the organization.

Third paragraph: Try to answer the question, why should I hire you? Emphasize the interests, skills, and personality traits that make you particularly well suited to the position. For example, "In addition to my accomplishments, I work well with little supervision, and I get along well with diverse groups of people."

Fourth paragraph: This is the closing. Say that you're very interested in the position and that you believe you would be of great value to the organization. Request a meeting; try to frame this in a way that makes the reader want to meet with you. Example: "I have some specific ideas for activities that I'd like to discuss with you. Could we set up a meeting?" Tell the person to whom you're writing when you'll follow up. Remember, always thank the potential employer.

Gaps in Employment

For anyone who has gaps in his or her work history, writing a resume and cover letter can be a difficult task. Gaps on a resume may be of concern because the potential employer may feel the applicant's skills are obsolete.

Today, the most overwhelming concern is familiarity with technology. Most applicants believe they can achieve that with increased training and practice. Whatever you've done between positions can be seen as helpful and beneficial if it is presented effectively. One strategy is to discuss and highlight in your cover letter your accomplishments during your time away and keep the focus on paid employment on the resume. Parents who have been out of the workplace for a while should highlight their time management or organizational and balancing skills. Others who have been out of the workplace should discuss their projects and experience in the most practical and meaningful way. For example, if you've participated in fundraising or community events, mention those.

Sample Cover Letter for an Advertised Position

Date

(contact name and address)
Ms. Jane Doe, Sales Manager
Retter Corporation
15th Street, NE
New York, New York 10025

Dear Ms. Doe:
In response to your May 5 advertisement in the *New York Times* for a part-time sales representative, I am enclosing my resume. My background and experience fit very closely with those stated in the advertisement.

For the past five years, I have been the sales manager of the sales division for the XYZ Corporation. For the last three years, everyone on the sales staff exceeded his or her goal by 15 percent. In addition, I was responsible for managing a staff of fifteen, and I designed a new sales incentive program for the company.

At this point in my career, I am interested in working part-time in sales. As you can see from my resume, my background is well suited for the position.

I am very interested in pursuing this position and would greatly appreciate the opportunity to discuss it with you. I will call you next Thursday to follow up. In the meantime, feel free to call me at xxx-xxx-xxxx. Thank you for your time and consideration.

Sincerely,

Sample Targeted Mailing

Date

Mr. X, President
McQuinn Corporation
10 Bradley Boulevard
Washington, D.C. 20036

Dear Mr. X,
I recently read a newspaper article describing your company's expansion. It is apparent that your company is growing, and I am very excited about its future prospects. I believe I could be of tremendous value to you as part of your sales division.

As you can see on my resume, I have been involved in several facets of your business, including working closely with the banking industry. I've worked extensively in marketing and sales, with significant accomplishments in my division. Recently, I was named most creative on my team and received an industry award.

I am an enthusiastic team player with a results-oriented approach to business. I appreciate and respect your company's values of hard work, responsibility, and loyalty.

I would appreciate the opportunity to meet with you to discuss possibilities for working part-time or on a consultant basis with your company. I believe my background, skills, and interests are an ideal fit for your organization. I will call you next week to arrange an appointment.

Thank you for your time and consideration.

Sincerely,

_____

(Note: For either cover letter, you could choose to highlight your accomplishments in a bulleted format, which would replace paragraphs two and three in the sample cover letters.)

Follow-Up

Follow-up is crucial to securing any job. It shows persistence, interest, and old-fashioned courtesy. All of these qualities are well respected and appreciated in the workplace. If you don't hear back after your initial follow-up, try again, as long as enough time has gone by between your follow-up calls, emails, or letters. It's good practice to let a week go by between follow-up calls. Studies indicate that it can take as many as eight attempts to follow up and elicit the interest of the person you're trying to contact. I believe that's a bit extreme, and I don't recommend it because you risk becoming a pest. I do embrace the belief, however, that you need to try at least a few times. Many people get distracted and actually appreciate your repeated efforts to reach them.

Preparing for Job Interviews

Employers have a few major concerns, and it's crucial that you address them during an interview. They include:

- Is this person capable of doing the job? (Skills or transferable skills, related experience)
- How inspired is the person to do the job? (Motivation, work habits, interest)
- Will this person fit in? (Personality style and similar value system preference)

The more prepared you are for the interview, the easier it will be for you. As the interviewee, your job is to convince the interviewer that you're able to do the job and that you want it. Most important, you need to describe key accomplishments that demonstrate this. Let the interviewer know that you have researched the company and feel you will fit in. Also communicate to the interviewer that you value what his or her company does.

Think carefully about what makes you unique. What do

you have to offer in the way of experience, background, education, and personality? What is your edge or unique selling point? As a part-timer, think about the employer's potential concerns and address them (see chapter 5 for tips on countering employer objections).

You can differentiate yourself from others interviewing for the same position by being adequately prepared. To communicate effectively during an interview, you must be able to answer the following questions:

- Why are you looking for a job? That is, are you reentering the market or leaving one company for another?
- Why did you seek a position with us?
- What are the most important rewards you expect in your job?
- What are your short- and long-term plans?
- What qualifications do you have that you believe will make you successful in this job?
- What value can you add to this company/organization?
- What two or three accomplishments are you most proud of?
- What would your past colleagues or supervisors say about you?
- What would your friends say about you?
- Why do you want to work part-time?
- What are your special strengths?

Note: Sometimes an interviewer simply says, "So, tell me about yourself." You can use this list of questions to formulate a response.

WHAT ARE YOUR GREATEST WEAKNESSES?

This is one of the most feared interview questions. It's best to describe one of your strengths as if it were a weakness. Any exaggerated strength can be turned into a weakness. For example, many people describe their perfectionism; they work too hard, etc. If you honestly feel your weaknesses are minimal, you can say that to the interviewer. For example, "I understand your concerns; however, regarding this position, I don't believe I have anything that would get in the way of my performing a good job for you."

Another approach is to explain a specific situation and let the interviewer know that you learned from the experience and that your level of self-awareness and accountability has increased as a result of the incident, and you won't make the same mistake twice. But be careful using this technique; you don't want to supply negative information. The mistake should be relatively minor, but the learning opportunity significant.

Additional questions along this line include:

- Who has been the most difficult person for you to work with? The easiest?
- How do you work under stress?

HOW WOULD YOU DEAL WITH THIS SITUATION? (THE INTERVIEWER DESCRIBES A POTENTIAL SITUATION AT WORK)

This is more of a behavioral interview question. Try to draw on experiences where you've been successful in a similar situation. If you can't think of an example, let the interviewer know that you are resourceful and able to think quickly. The more you brainstorm questions, the more prepared you'll be for whatever the interviewer springs on you.

Try to remember that the underlying question to answer during an interview is, "Why should I hire you?" Your job is to alleviate any doubt by letting the interviewer know that you are very interested, have a motivated skill to do the job, feel you would fit in, and would be proud to be affiliated with the organization.

Attitude is key. Try to be as enthusiastic as possible. Practice, practice, practice. The more you practice, the better you'll be. Do mock interviews with a friend, family member, or career coach until you feel comfortable. The interviewer will sense your confidence. One of the best strategies is to remember that you are interviewing the company as much as the interviewer is interviewing you. You want to make the best match possible, so you need to listen and ask appropriate questions to determine this. Here are some sample questions you can ask the interviewer when it's your turn:

- Why is this job open?
- How long was the last person in this job?
- Why did that person leave?
- Is there anything you would like to change from how the job was typically done?
- What would you like me to accomplish immediately? In three months? In six?
- What is a typical day like?
- How many people would I work with?
- Who would my manager/boss be?
- How much autonomy would I have in the job?
- How would I be evaluated? When? How often?
- What makes someone successful in this job?
- What are the ideal characteristics someone would possess to do this job well?

Presenting Yourself in the Best Way

Believe it or not, most interviewers decide within fifteen seconds of meeting you. It's crucial that you appear organized, professional, and enthusiastic. You must be well groomed—clothes clean and neat, hair cut and/or styled. If you're a man, shave or neatly trim a beard or mustache. Follow the dress code for the organization. Even if it's casual—for example, you know most people there wear jeans to work—you may want to step it up to khakis. The exception would be if you are interviewing for a wildly creative company that prides itself on originality. But this is the rare exception and not the rule. When in doubt, dress conservatively.

Body language is important, so you should stand up tall and try not to seem tense. Arrive early so you can take a few minutes to collect yourself. Breathe deeply and try to get into a relaxed state before the interview. You might want to spend the time observing the company and any written materials that might be available. Try hard not to fidget, tap your feet, or play with your hair, a pen, or change in your pockets.

Try to appear calm during the interview. Slow down. Your voice can be heard best at a natural pace and medium volume. Be energetic and not phony. Show that you have good listening skills and maintain sufficient eye contact. Look interested and engaged, smile and nod as appropriate, follow the interviewer's lead. Do not interrupt. It may be good to let the interviewer see your thoughtfulness, so a moment of silence is fine after a specific, thought-provoking question. If you do not know something, say so. The interviewer will appreciate your honesty.

Different Interview Formats

Sometimes the interviewer is more nervous than the interviewee. You may be interviewed by a novice who has no idea what a good interview entails. This type of interview can be very casual and open-ended. This, in fact, can be very hard for the interviewee, as you may need to lead and be more direct to make sure the interviewer understands your qualifications and interests.

More typical is a planned and organized interview. It usually starts with small talk and an icebreaker, then you'll be asked to talk about your background and qualifications (this is where your personal pitch comes in handy). The interviewer will ask questions about your strengths and weaknesses. There is time for the interviewee to ask questions at the end. Always conclude with a thank you and ask about next steps.

There are certain illegal questions that the interviewer cannot ask. These include marital status, family size, religion, your credit rating, and other personal questions. It's certainly your right to refuse to answer, but if you're still interested in the position, be tactful about dodging the question. For example, if someone asks you if you're planning to start a family, you could avoid the question by saying, "I'm focused on my career right now and excited about this opportunity."

Follow up within forty-eight hours of your meeting. If you didn't get the chance to say something during the interview, now you have an opportunity to address it. In your follow-up letter or note, thank the individual for your time together, mention any pertinent information that you forgot during the initial interview, restate your interest and enthusiasm, and once again let the person know why he or she should hire you.

Try to listen very carefully during an interview. It's very easy in such situations to miss crucial information about the job because you think you want the job very much. For example, a client of mine got a very sought-after job and was thrilled. During the interview, the interviewer told her there would be a lot of writing involved. Deep down she knew she didn't want to spend all her time writing, but the company was so well known and respected that she tuned out this information. As it turned out, she spent a very short time at the company because it ended up not being a good fit for her motivated skills. Try to be as honest with yourself as possible about your motivated skills and interest in the job and avoid being influenced by other secondary factors.

Even if you don't get the job, you can always learn things about yourself for future interviews. Immediately following an interview write down your initial impressions. They are usually correct. Think about what went well, what didn't go well, and what you would do differently next time. What questions made you nervous? Ask yourself is this truly a good fit. Will this job satisfy my needs? How was my body language? Answers to these questions will provide valuable insight into what you need to work on and pay attention to in future interviews.

References

Establishing and maintaining your list of references is an ongoing process, as you will need them in the future. This is one of the reasons you need to keep in touch with the people you use as references and keep them abreast of your current situation. If you do this periodically, you won't feel awkward when you need to call these people to ask for a reference in the future.

When deciding whom to use for references, choose people who appreciate your talents, experience, and character. Try to select people who add credibility to the position for which you're applying.

The purpose of a reference check is to add validity to your qualifications and to verify information. Recruiters and hiring managers use it to reconfirm their belief that you can do the job. It can be a simple check of employment dates or a more thorough examination of your strengths and weaknesses. Many employers also run a background check to make sure you don't have a criminal record or credit problems. I know of a few clients (in the field of finance) who lost opportunities due to a bad credit history.

Usually you need to supply the names of two or three references. Think carefully about your choices. The best potential choices are:

- present or former bosses,
- colleagues,
- people who know your abilities from a professional or volunteer association,
- anyone who can speak to your integrity and character, and
- college contacts or professors.

Obviously, if you're changing positions and want to keep it confidential, don't ask your current employer to be a reference.

Your goal is to maximize the value of each reference. Therefore, it's important to coach your reference on what skills to emphasize. Most potential references appreciate advice about what to say and what to highlight; after all, they may not have worked with you in a while. Let them know what you'd like them to emphasize with regard to strengths, skills, and abilities, accomplishments, and character. Be as specific as possible. If you want them to mention a particular accomplishment, skill, or personality trait, say so. References might also be asked if the person being discussed has any problem areas or areas that need improvement. Be careful with this. You may want to give your reference some potential answers to difficult questions or at least suggest that they tactfully sidestep such questions.

Once you've finished "coaching" your references, make sure they feel comfortable with the information. Let them know how important their recommendations are and how much you appreciate their help.

Potential employers usually don't like letters of reference, and it's best not to offer references until asked. Once someone asks for references, call these people immediately so they are prepared.

Even if you don't get the position, let references who were contacted know what happened and thank them. You might need to ask them for another reference, or they might have other additional ideas for you to explore. And remember, they may need you some day as well. If you get the chance to do someone a favor, leap at the opportunity.

Make it as easy as possible for the person checking the reference. List names, the nature of your relationship to that person, and current mailing and email addresses and phone numbers.

Negotiating Your Salary

See the section in chapter 5 on Tips for Negotiating Compensation.

Sample Functional Resume

JOHN DOE

Web Site: www.johndoe.com
E-mail: johndoe123@gmail.com

123 Main Street, Apartment 8N   (574) 265-9874 (Home)
New York, New York 10021   (917) 654-2579 (Mobile)

SUMMARY

Sales/marketing executive with experience in sales and market planning, development, and research. Highly skilled communicator who has shown exemplary interpersonal and management skills to achieve increased profits and productivity.

SALES

- Hired and oversaw a sales support team of 25 individuals. Worked with clients such as the *Wall Street Journal*, AMEX, and major banks. Managed 70 accounts per year; 90% met or exceeded expectations.
- Managed telecommunications sales representatives. Surpassed customer service and sales productivity projections for two years.

MARKETING

- Directed the sales, research, and marketing efforts.
- Recruited and managed staff of 10, plus consultants, to develop initial market plan for the industry. Project, which included strategies and applications, was delivered to seven operating units.

MANAGEMENT

- Reestablished work processes, increasing productivity and reducing expenses by $1M. Received award for this effort.
- Initiated and directed transition for employees' selection and marketing sales efforts for 23 operating companies.

CAREER HIGHLIGHTS

XYZ CORPORATION, New York, NY
Director, Market Planning
1988–Present
Hired staff to develop market plans for six entire markets representing 60% of business revenues of 4.0.B: Banking, Securities, Insurance Professional Services, Distribution, Health Care, and Education.

Director, Planning, Government Affairs
Directed all operations for the department. Managed a $6M budget and 30 employees plus consultants.

ABC COMMUNICATIONS RESEARCH, Trenton, NJ
1984–1988

Division Manager/Marketing Manager
Market division manager with a staff of 11 and a budget of $3M, worked on consultative market research support for seven Regional Operating Companies on concerns involving the use of third parties to market products and services.

CDE COMPANY, Newark, NJ
1982–1984
District Manager Marketing Operations
Initiated and managed all marketing operations planning for the companies.

Staff Manager Product Marketing
Developed product marketing materials for the new product plans and presented them to all 23 telephone companies.

CDE COMPANY, New York, NY
Before 1982
Sales Manager
Directed a group of account executives who sold products and service to markets within the telecommunication industry. Exceeded objectives for five years.

EDUCATION
M.B.A., Marketing, Baruch College, New York, NY
B.A., Economics, Cornell University, Ithaca, NY
Executive Management Courses:
University of Michigan, Ann Arbor, MI
New York University
Columbia University, New York, NY

AWARDS
Government Affairs Quality Award, 1992–1993
President's Quality Award, 1993

COMMUNITY SERVICE
Board member, local Y, volunteer in senior center

REFERENCES:
References will be furnished upon request.

Sample Chronological Resume

JOHN DOE
Web Site: www.johndoe.com
E-mail: johndoe123@gmail.com

123 Main Street, Apartment 8N	(574) 265-9874 (Home)
New York, New York 10021	(917) 654-2579 (Mobile)

PROFESSIONIAL EXPERIENCE

CAREER COACH, New York, NY   1990–Present
- Coach individuals to clarify career and life concerns using personalized assessment materials, including standard vocational tests.
- Create plans and objectives with clients to help them achieve their goals.
- Work with executives to help them maximize their effectiveness in the workplace.

CAREER INFORMATION SPECIALIST,
Center for Career and Life Planning   1990–1992
New York, New York

- Assisted clients to explore research materials relating to their Strong Interest Inventory®.
- Categorized reference and materials in career library.

ASSOCIATE CONSULTANT, XYZ Company
New York, New York   1988–1989
- Consulted and solved problems on various compensation issues for client companies.
- Designed executive compensation and salary administration programs.

HUMAN RESOURCE CONSULTANT/COMPENSATION ANALYST
ABC Insurance Company, New York, New York   1984–1988
- Recruited exempt and nonexempt personnel, saving the company $75,000 in 1985.
- Conducted research to develop new employee programs, e.g., Company Wellness Programs, Employee Assessment and Testing.
- Set salaries for new employees.

- Evaluated exempt and nonexempt jobs in accordance with established evaluation system.

PLACEMENT COUNSELOR, FGE personnel
New York, New York   1981–1982
- Interviewed and assessed prospective applicants.
- Prepared applicants for job interviews.
- Developed and maintained relationships.

EDUCATION
Columbia University, New York, New York, Ed. M. in Counseling Psychology, 1990
Columbia University, New York, New York, M.A. in Organizational Psychology, 1984
University of Vermont, Burlington VT, B.S. in Business Administration, 1980

PROFESSIONAL AFFILIATIONS
NATIONAL CERTIFIED COUNSELOR/PROFESSIONAL CERTIFIED COACH:
- Member Board of Directors, local Y
- Association of Career Professionals International
- Career Development Specialists Network
- International Coach Federation
- Former Co-Host Career SIG Coach University

REFERENCES
References will be furnished upon request

Books on Resume Writing

- *101 Best.com Resumes and Cover Letters*, Jay Block, 2001
- *Arco 7-Minute Resumes*, Dana Morgan, 2000
- *Best Resumes for $100,000+ Jobs*, Wendy Enelow, 2002
- *Building a Great Resume*, Kate Wendleton, 1999
- *The Complete Idiot's Guide to the Perfect Resume*, Susan Ireland, 2000
- *Cyberspace Resume Kit*, Fred E. Jandt and Mary B. Nemnich, 2001

- *The Edge: Resume and Job Search Strategy*, Bill Corbin, 2000
- *Electronic Resumes and Online Networking*, Rebecca Smith, 2000
- *E-Resumes: Everything You Need to Know about Using Electronic Resumes to Tap into Today's Job Market*, Susan Whitcomb, 2002
- *The Everything Resume Book*, Stanley Graber, 2000
- *The Federal Resume Guidebook*, Kathryn Troutman, 1999
- *Gallery of Best Resumes for People Without a Four-Year Degree*, Davis Noble, 2000
- *The Global Resume and CV Guide*, Mary Anne Thompson, 2000
- *High Impact Resumes and Letters*, Ronald Krannich, 2006
- *The Insider's Guide to Writing the Perfect Resume*, Karl Weber, 2001
- *Packaging Yourself: The Targeted Resume*, Kate Wendleton, 2005
- *The Resume.com Guide to Writing Unbeatable Resumes*, by Warren Simons and Rose Curtis, 2004.
- *The Resume Kit*, 4th ed., Richard Beatty, 2000
- *Resume Magic: Trade Secrets of a Professional Resume Writer*, Susan Britton Whitcomb, 2003
- *Resumes in Cyberspace*, Pat Criscito, 2000
- *Resumes that Knock 'Em Dead*, Martin Yate, 2002
- *Writing a Great Resume: Career Success in under 100 Pages*, Peter Weddle, 2002

Books on Cover Letters

- *7-Minute Cover Letters*, Dana Morgan, 2000
- *Adams Cover Letter Almanac*, Richard Wallace, 2006
- *Cover Letter Magic*, Wendy S. Enelow, 2004
- *Cover Letters that Knock 'Em Dead*, Martin Yate, 6th ed., 2004
- *The Everything Cover Letter Book*, Steven Graber, 2000
- *Haldane's Best Cover Letters for Professionals*, Bernard Haldane Associates, 2000
- *Nail the Cover Letter: Great Tips for Creating Dynamite Letters*, Ron Krannich, 2005

CHAPTER 11

Tools for Success: Personal, Office, and Business Needs

Congratulations, You Have Achieved Your Goal

There are three main ways to prepare yourself to be a successful part-time professional: take care of your personal needs, take care of your office needs (whether you work out of your home or an office), and take care of your financial and business needs (preparing for taxes, insurance, and retirement).

Personal Needs

I'm starting with personal needs, because as you probably realize by now, I believe that happiness is rooted in your personal experience and in the balance you can achieve between life needs and work needs.

A Simple Prescription for Everyday Success

I ask my clients to come up with five to ten healthy habits they can do daily or weekly to keep them physically, mentally, spiritually, and emotionally well. When you're in good shape in these key areas, you're better able to make assessments about your life and situation. For example, do you need quiet time? Say twenty minutes a day to meditate, pray, or simply have a peaceful, quiet break? Figure out when, how, and where you're going to do this.

Are you someone who needs a complete day—for example, Sunday—with absolutely nothing to do? Or can you be productive seven days a week working in shorter sprints?

Is your appearance important to you? Do you need time for manicures, haircuts, clothes shopping? Don't forget time for relationships, including leisurely phone calls to friends and relatives? How about sex with your significant other? When are you going to have time for that?

My point is that we have to give these things thought or they will lurk at the bottom of our "things to do" list. Ignoring these issues will cause you problems in the long run, while taking care of them will give you comfort and pleasure. So, pick up a pencil and paper or log onto your computer and start planning. It's your time—but it's precious and limited, so you must budget it.

Personal Needs/Values Exercise

We all have personal needs and values that must be satisfied for us to be happy. They're essential to enable us to get through the day. These are things you must have or feel. Be clear about what they are. Rank the following as follows: 1, not very important; 2, somewhat important; 3, very important. If you don't see a "need" or "value" that's important to you, add it to the list. I need:

- to be well regarded
- to be independent
- to have a task or duty
- to be accepted
- to accomplish
- to be acknowledged
- to be right
- to be cared for
- to feel a sense of certainty

- to be comfortable
- to feel good physically
- to look good
- to communicate
- to be needed
- to feel loved
- to be free
- to have fun
- to be honest

- to have a creative outlet—
  art, music
- to be with my family
- to be safe
- to feel balanced
- to feel financially secure
- to be rested
- to work
- to worship

- order
- peace
- excitement
- power
- sex
- time alone—
  read, meditate
- movement, exercise
- friendship

Try to be aware of your needs and values and be as proactive as possible in meeting them so you're not frustrated when you don't get them. For example, if you need feedback and communication, ask for it from friends and loved ones or colleagues and bosses on a reasonable, consistent basis. When you take more responsibility for your needs, you'll feel better about your situation.

Organize and Prioritize

Knowing what you want and need out of life is of the utmost importance, but organizing and prioritizing what you do during your day/week/month/year is also key. We already did a bit of this when we looked at healthy habits and personal needs/ values. I recommend that you take care of yourself first. If you feel guilty about this because you have needy family members, think of it this way: it's similar to the instructions flight attendants give passengers about oxygen masks. They instruct parents to place the oxygen mask over their faces first, so they don't collapse and become unable to assist their children.

It's also similar to the advice for entrepreneurs: pay yourself first. So, as you think about organizing and prioritizing, I want you to do just that—take care of your personal needs first.

That said, as a Savvy Part-Time Professional you're going to set up systems and structures to help you deal with your multiple demands. You need to streamline things like grocery

(Continued on page 243)

Sample Savvy Part-time Professional Schedule Chart

Monday	Tuesday	Wednesday	Thursday	Friday
▪ Day off: workout/ exercise		▪ Early morning workout/exercise		▪ Early morning workout/ exercise
▪ Take care of household finances ▪ Pay bills	▪ Workday	▪ Workday	▪ Workday	▪ Workday
▪ Schedule doctor, dentist visits if necessary	▪ Call a friend or family member	▪ Look at overall financial health: taxes, insurance, retirement planning	▪ If you're an entrepreneur or consultant, examine your finances once a week	▪ Personal treat, for example, haircut, manicure, massage, etc.
▪ Spend quality time with children and/or elderly relatives ▪ Take a personal development class or seek additional training ▪ Family dinner	▪ Family dinner	▪ Work dinner or dinner with friends or family	▪ Date night with significant other	▪ Family dinner

(Continued from page 241)

shopping and cooking. And give this one considerable thought because you don't want to fall into bad eating habits, which leads to a host of other problems. Who's going to do the shopping/cooking and when? Can you have some things delivered regularly? Can you have a pizza night? Can you take turns with other household members? Check out the finance information in chapter 2 to keep control of expenses.

If you have children, you have to work out their schedules very carefully. My advice here is that you have backup plan after backup plan. In other words, if you're stuck in traffic and you can't pick up the kids, whom do you call? If that person isn't available, who's next on your list, and so on and so on?

Figure out the best time or day for maintenance work, whether it's for your house, your pet, or yourself, for example, regular medical and dental appointments for you and your family.

Remember, no one is going to figure this stuff out for you. When you take the time to take care of these details before an emergency, you'll much better equipped mentally and emotionally to succeed at work and at home. So take a day—a vacation day, a personal day, a Sunday—to brainstorm your schedule and backup plans.

It's All in Your Attitude

Be open to new experiences and new people. Be aware of the words you use; they define how you think. It can be helpful to

---

Schedule Tip

As a Savvy Part-Time Professional, your goal is to set up your schedule for success. Therefore, if possible, try to take Mondays off. You'll have a more restful weekend, and you'll feel less pressure to work additional hours. The logic behind this is as follows: if Friday is your day off, and a project is extended later in the week, you may feel pressured to work that extra day.

understand and appreciate the value of the words you use. Try to replace negative words with positive or neutral words. For example, the expressions "I will," "I can," "I agree," etc., can make a difference.

The people with whom you spend time can greatly influence your mood and attitude. When you start spending time with people who have taken risks and have made career decisions similar to yours, you'll feel supported and enriched. Read inspiring books about people who have made interesting career decisions and conquered challenges. Biographies of people you admire can be quite helpful. If reading is not your preference, listen to individuals being interviewed on the radio, the television, or on books on tape.

Get involved—explore and discover. This will keep you fresh and give you things to look forward to as a reward for your hard work and efforts.

Office Needs

SETTING UP YOUR FIRST HOME OFFICE

First, think about how you work best. Think about all the supplies you'll need. In addition to the standard ones such as pens, paper clips, stapler, etc., you need to determine how you want to organize your office. For example, do you want a file cabinet or storage boxes? Blackboard or bulletin board? Do you prefer to keep your work surface clear? If so, you might want to consider shelving or racks for files and storage. What type of desk? Will you use primarily a laptop or a desktop computer? Don't forget that you'll need room for a printer and a fax machine. You might check out one or two office superstores to see what's available and if they deliver. Many have departments geared specifically to the home office.

Second, where will your office be? This is critical. Have you designated a separate area in your home? It must be free from noise and distractions, and being able to close your door for privacy is a plus. Many people forget about good lighting, but this is very important to avoid unnecessary eyestrain.

Third, a comfortable chair is a necessity. Think ergonomically and pay attention to the distance between the computer and your chair. Remember, a good chair is a worthwhile investment because it can prevent chronic back pain.

Fourth, an excellent phone system, office-oriented software, and high-speed Internet connection are essential. Buy a computer with a lot of memory and save or back up your documents regularly. You definitely want to have the name of several reliable computer services on file. That way, if your computer crashes, you'll have someone to call immediately. If you're working with or for one company, you can try to negotiate equipment acquisition and servicing with that organization. If you're on your own, you have to factor all this into your business plan.

Finally, decide if you need outside support; this could be an administrative assistant, file clerk, errand person, etc. Take your time deciding what type of help you need and consider the attendant cost and space requirements.

When you hire other people, look for individuals who share your philosophy toward a healthy work/life balance. What you can offer them in flexible and pleasant work conditions might make up for a smaller paycheck.

TIPS FOR AVOIDING CLUTTER

Unless you're a carefree, easygoing, high-tolerance person, clutter has a way of causing subconscious stress. Get in the habit of being ruthless about "stuff," for both work and home. Establish a system for going through email and snail mail quickly. Have a trash/recycle pile as well as a high- and medium-priority pile. Set up multiple folders for your email so you don't have a long list of things bugging you.

Here's my trick: anything that's low priority should go in the trash/recycle. Face it, you're unlikely to get to it, and by the time you do, it will be out of date. In the electronic age, you can almost always find what you're looking for on the Internet if you decide down the road you really did need that catalog or form letter. Keep a good email address book—that way you can contact people whenever you need to without hunting down old emails.

Same with your closets and cupboards. If you don't wear it or use it, give it away or throw it away. But don't let the give-aways pile up. If you don't want it, does someone else? This is especially true for clothes.

If in doubt about whether you want to keep something or throw it out, do a tryout. Wear the item for a day. Did you like it? If not, get rid of it. Pick up the magazine or journal that's been cluttering up your office. Anything interesting? Does it make you feel good or bad to flip through it? If in doubt, throw it out.

Visit www.flylady.com for tips on organizing.

SETTING BOUNDARIES

It's very important to set boundaries if you work at home. Although it can be difficult, you must be as clear about your working hours as if you were working in an office building. For example, for the past fifteen years, I've had an office outside my home as well as one at home. My family understands that when my door is closed, I'm working, and unless it's an emergency, they are not to disturb me.

Those who work at home also find that friends and neighbors sometimes take advantage of the situation by asking for favors during the workday. You need to let people know that just because you're home, it doesn't mean you're free to do someone else's errands, babysit children, or walk the dog. Communicate your needs and boundaries clearly.

Tips for Working in an Organization

Now that you've achieved your goal of securing a good part-time position, here are some tips to get you started:

- Research and read everything you can about the company or organization. If there's a description of your job, review it carefully.

- It's helpful to connect with other individuals who work at the company part-time; get to know them and ask about their successes and challenges.
- Orient yourself to the organization's people, challenges, systems, and procedures. Have a conversation with your new boss and ask such questions as:

  - "Is there anything significant and current occurring in the organization of which I need to be aware?"
  - "Who are the key people I should know? Which administrative people should I meet?"
  - "What procedures and official meeting requirements might be relevant to my work?"

- Agree on a schedule of activities for the first thirty days and an abbreviated thirty- or sixty-day review to see how you're doing.
- Find out how your boss prefers you to communicate with him or her (phone, email, memos).
- Ask your peers and colleagues about their current activities, backgrounds, and experience. Develop a network of individuals with whom you feel comfortable and find a mentor if possible. Become a team player; try to identify the company's formal and informal communications network—written, verbal, and the "grapevine." Be a good listener and pay attention to your surroundings. Recognize the priorities of the organization and your department.
- Let your peers and colleagues know you'll be working part-time so there will be no surprises later on. Make sure everyone knows your schedule.
- Try to schedule lunch with others on your days in the office, so you hear about any information or changes that occur on your days off.
- Try to be as helpful as possible. Become visible even if you are only there part-time. If invited, try to participate in company functions, for example, picnics, parties, and athletic

activities.

- Be aware of your conduct; be respectful of and loyal to your boss.
- Dress appropriately; pay careful attention to the dress code, both written and observed.
- Try not to make judgments for the first four to six months; let yourself settle in first.
- I recommend that my clients keep an accomplishment folder and include notes on successful experiences. You are your best advocate; you need to remember all your successes and share them when appropriate.
- Be clear about how and when you are evaluated. After you receive your first evaluation, do any matters need to be renegotiated?
- Maintain a positive attitude. Try to focus at work and leave personal problems at home.
- Maintain a professional posture and take pride in doing a good job. You'll feel better, and others will respect you. This kind of attitude and work ethic will also help you advance or move to another position, career, or company.
- Remember, your boss is going to try to be your best supporter. He or she selected you and wants you to succeed, since it reflects on him or her. Maintain a win-win posture.

Career Management

Periodically review your career—where you are and where you want to be in five years and ten years. For example, how do you plan to build on your strengths? Are there any additional skills you'd like or need to develop to help you as a part-time professional? For example, developing solid negotiation skills is essential. Do you have any additional career plans? If so, you may want to analyze your situation and determine what your next course of action should be. As mentioned previously, it's always a good practice to maintain an accomplishment folder to highlight your successes.

Build a sold network of contacts and stay in touch with them. Let them know how your job is going and what you're planning for the future. Ask for feedback from your boss and colleagues. If you're involved in a large organization, reach out to other departments to learn what they do. In this way you'll build your knowledge base and get ideas for the future.

Don't Forget to Reward Yourself

Now that you've transitioned successfully to your new situation, congratulate yourself. You've conquered this transition, and there will be many more in your work and life to come. The processes and learning you have acquired will serve you well, and you'll be able to help others going through a similar change.

As you move forward, make sure you take time to appreciate and reflect on your achievements. Try to manage your finances well so you can plan short- and long-term rewards for your various accomplishments, big and small.

- Short-term reward: go out for a nice lunch or dinner, take a personal day, go on a weekend getaway, treat yourself to a day at the spa, buy yourself something you've wanted for a long time.

- Long-term reward: take the vacation you've always dreamed about or purchase a longed-for item—a car, a home renovation, a new wardrobe.

Financial Needs: Taxes, Savings, and Retirement

Taxes, savings, and retirement are huge issues that are outside the scope of this book. In fact, entire books have been written about each subject. Nevertheless, you must consider each of these carefully as you start your part-time career.

It is especially important that freelancers, consultants, contract workers, and entrepreneurs understand their tax situation. If you find yourself in one of these categories, you need to be

(Continued on page 251)

Schedule Creep and Schedule Burnout

Avoid the dreaded "schedule creep."* This is a true hazard for part-time professionals. When work backs up, employers or clients will try to get you to work beyond your scheduled hours for no additional pay. You may have to "pitch in" some extra hours every once in a while, but if you find yourself working almost a full-time schedule for only half-time pay, you're doing yourself a grave disservice. At that point, you'll be tempted to leave the position or go back to full-time work under the assumption that if you're virtually working full-time, you might as well get paid for full-time. And there goes your work/life balance. You'll find yourself right back on the hamster wheel you tried so hard to escape. Stick to your scheduled hours, learn how to say no, or demand more money for the "extra" work.

Also avoid "schedule burnout." Sometimes out of ignorance, lack of organization, or thriftiness, your office may expect you to complete a full-time workload in part-time hours, and you'll drive yourself crazy trying to get everything done in the allotted time. If you find this happening, it's time to talk to your supervisor to set more realistic expectations. It's simply impossible to do five days of work in three. No one can keep that up —you'll burn out.

As a Savvy Part-Time Professional, you have to be highly focused and productive at work. You also have to be disciplined and confident enough to stick to your boundaries. Work on your time management and negotiating skills and build up your confidence so you can say no or renegotiate when necessary.

* According to an article in the *Wall Street Journal* by Sue Shellenbarger, the term, "schedule creep," as it relates to part-timers, was coined by Joan Williams, director of the Project for Attorney Retention at American University (www.pardc.org). It's a term "she borrowed from the construction industry."

(Continued from page 249)

proactive and set aside money for taxes; in fact, you have to pay estimated quarterly taxes. It's very hard to allocate money for taxes, especially if you're accustomed to having a company do it for you. Jill Feldman, a CPA tax and financial adviser in New York City, recommends setting up a separate bank account. A safe amount to allocate is 30 percent of your income. Refer to www.irs.gov/businesses/small and a qualified tax accountant for more information. Related professional associations are also good sources for tips and helpful information. Remember, when it comes to taxes, the Internal Revenue Service (IRS) is the ultimate authority. You may need help understanding the regulations. If so, get that help.

If you're self-employed, a business owner, or have a home-based office, you also need to be careful about deductions as you may be flagged for audits. Check with the IRS and a qualified accountant to make sure you are taking the deductions you deserve and not claiming deductions that will come back to haunt you.

Those who work part-time, especially those without such retirement benefits as a 401(k), need to take a proactive approach to saving. Financial adviser Jill Feldman suggests thinking of it as a pie whose pieces include retirement, savings, and taxes. In my opinion, the best course of action to prepare you for wise financial planning is to speak to a professional tax planner, accountant, or investment adviser.

Health Insurance

If you're not covered through work or through a family policy, you need to secure coverage. Whenever I talk with people about working independently, they demonstrate a great deal of uncertainly and anxiety about this issue. Choosing a health insurance plan is a very important and personal choice. You should be very clear about your needs, research your options very carefully, and shop around for the best plan. The cost varies depending on your age, medical history, and the insurer you select. Take the time to compare prices and plans. An insurance agent can help you wade through the many choices. Even though detailed insurance matters are beyond the scope of this book, here are some quick points to consider.

If you are an independent or one-person business, a standard individual or family policy is best. If you're anticipating a short-term situation, you should purchase a temporary policy. If you're a group of a few employees, or you can get a group policy through an association, a group policy is better. There are also tax savings to self-employed health insurance costs. The laws and regulations are subject to change, so you should contact your tax accountant or financial adviser for the specifics, and contact an insurance agent for information about the health plan that's right for you.

A valuable alternative available for those leaving a company policy is COBRA. COBRA (which stands for Consolidated Omnibus Budget Reconciliation Act) is a law that requires companies with more than twenty employees to offer employees who leave the option of receiving continuing coverage through the company insurance plan for eighteen months. It can be expensive since the employee must pay the full premium, plus up to 2 percent in administrative expenses. I recommend that all my clients consider this option carefully when leaving an organization. At least your coverage is properly taken care of, and you have time to shop around for other less expensive options in the meantime.

Other Insurance Needs: Disability and Life

If you become ill or are injured, it's best to have disability insurance, which covers unexpected costs and lost wages. You need to research and compare prices for disability insurance and for life insurance. Everyone has his or her individual life insurance needs and budgets, but the rule of thumb is to get three to five times your annual salary in life insurance coverage.

Further Sources of Insurance or Insurance Information

There are many, many insurance carriers and resources on the Web; here are some ideas and links to get you started on your search. Investigate each site thoroughly before making any decisions. It's a good idea to check with your state attorney general's office and the Better Business Bureau, www.bbb.org, to see if any complaints have been filed against the carriers you're considering. To find the contact information for your state attorney general's office, visit the National Association of Attorney Generals Web site, www.naag.org.

- Associations. Group rates may be available through an association. Consult the *Encyclopedia of Associations*, available at libraries, for associations in your field. See chapter 6 for more links to associations.
- Businesses. Some associations provide benefits to small businesses. This is beneficial because you can get lower rates if you're part of a larger group. Some places to contact are:

  - The Small Business Benefits Association, www.sbba.com
  - United States Federation of Small Business, www.usfsb.com; the federation's insurance clearinghouse allows you to search using geography and other criteria.

- The American Benefits Association, www.abbcinc.com, bills itself as a "collection of individuals and groups who are uninsured, under insured, uninsurable or who just cannot afford a full blown health plan."
- Government sites. Go to the official Web site of your state government and do a keyword search under "insurance." Most states have an "insurance bureau" that is responsible for making sure that insurance companies are financially sound; that agents selling company policies are qualified;

and that insurance policies are of high quality, understandable, and fairly priced.

- The Home Office Association of America, www.hoaa.com
- www.healthinsuranceindepth.com; resources for understanding insurance and links to quotes for insurance
- www.unicare.com; provides plans for health care coverage

Unemployment Insurance for Part-Time Workers

According to a 2005 report by the National Employment Law Project, about half the states have policies that give part-time workers eligibility for unemployment insurance; however, requirements vary. Some reforms are underway to increase access to unemployment insurance for part-timers. Contact your local unemployment office for more information.

Life Is Short—Go for It!

Whether you're a baby boomer nearing retirement, a parent, or someone who simply wants more time to experience life, I hope that after reading *The Savvy Part-Time Professional* you feel you have the resources and encouragement to begin your search for a better work/life balance. I urge you to examine all of the options that will allow you to live your life in the most meaningful and fulfilling way. Life is too short and precious not to make the most of it.

SUGGESTED READING

Here are some recommended readings. Throughout the years, I have collected books worthy of inclusion in a bibliography of selected readings. Many of them are classics. They are separated into two sections: personal growth and career-related.

Personal Growth

Apter, Terry. *Working Women Don't Have Wives*, Palgrave Macmillian, 1995.

Bardwick, Judith. *The Plateauing Trap*, Bantam, 1988.

Bixler, Susan and Nancy Nix-Rice, *The Professional Image: Dress Your Best for Every Business Situation*, Adams Media Corp., 2005.

Bixler, Susan. *The Professional Presence*, Putnam, 1992.

Booher, Diana. *Getting a Life Without Sacrificing Your Career*, McGraw-Hill, 1996.

Borysenko, Joan. *Minding the Body, Mending the Mind*, Bantam, 1988.

Brandon, Nathaniel. *How to Raise Your Self-Esteem: The Proven Action-Oriented Approach to Greater Self-Respect and Self-Confidence*, Bantam, 1988.

Bravo, Ellen. *A 9 to 5 Guide to the Job/Family Challenge—Not for Women Only*, Wiley, 2005.

Bridges, William. *The Way of Transition: Embracing Life's Difficult Moments*, Perseus, 2000.

Burns, David. *Feeling Good: The New Mood Therapy*, Avon, 1999.

Burns, David. *The Feeling Good Handbook*, Plume, 1999.

Byalick, Marcia, and Linda Saslow. *The Three Career Couple: Mastering the Art of Juggling Work, Home, and Family*, Petersons, 1993.

Bykofsky, Sheree and Richard Carlson. *Me: Five Years from Now—The Life Planning Book You Write Yourself!* Hyperion, 1999.

Casey, Eileen L. *Maternity Leave—The Working Woman's Practical Guide to Combining Pregnancy, Motherhood & Career*, Green Mountain, 1992.

Caulfield, Jack, and Miller, Jacqueline (Eds.). *Heart at Work—Stories and Strategies for Building Self Esteem & Reawakening the Soul at Work*, McGraw-Hill, 1998.

Chopra, Deepak, M.D. *Ageless Body, Timeless Mind*, Harmony, 1994.

Clance, Pauline. *The Impostor Phenomenon: Overcoming the Fear That Haunts Your Success*, Peachtree, 1985.

Covey, Stephen. *The 7 Habits of Highly Effective People*, Free Press, 2004.

Cramer, Kathryn. *Staying on Top When Your World Turns Upside Down*, Viking, 1991.

Csikszentmihalyi, Mihalyi. *Flow: The Psychology of Optimal Experience*, HarperPerennial, 1991.

Ellis, Albert and William J. Knaus. *Overcoming Procrastination*, Signet, 1983.

Fields, Rick and editors of the New Age Journal. *Chop Wood, Carry Water: A Guide to Finding Spiritual Fulfillment in Everyday Life*, Tarcher, 1984.

Friedman, Martha. *Overcoming the Fear of Success*, Warner, 1988.

Galinsky, Ellen. *Ask the Children: The Breakthrough Study that Reveals How to Succeed at Work and Parenting*, Harper, 2000.

Gawain, Shakti. *A Creative Visualization: Use the Power of Your Imagination to Create What You Want in Your Life*, New World Library, 25th anniversary ed., 2002.

Goldberg, Philip. *The Intuitive Edge—Understanding & Developing Intuition*, Tarcher 1985.

Goleman, Daniel. *Emotional Intelligence*, 10th anniversary ed., Bantam, 2005.

Godfrey, Joline. *Our Wildest Dreams: Women Entrepreneurs Making Money, Having Fun, Doing Good*, Collins, 1993.

Gray, John. *Men Are from Mars, Women Are from Venus: A Practical Guide for Improving Communication and Getting What You Want in Your Relationships*, HarperCollins, 1993.

Handy, Charles. *The Age of Unreason*, Harvard Business School Press, 1998.

Harragan, Betty Lehan. *Games Mother Never Taught You*, Warner, 1989.

Helmstetter, Shad. *What to Say When You Talk to Yourself*, MJF Books, 1997.

Hendricks, Gary, and Ludeman, Kate. *The Corporate Mystic: A Guidebook for Visionaries with Their Feet on the Ground*, 1997.

Hyatt, Carole, and Linda Gottlieb. *When Smart People Fail: Rebuilding Yourself for Success*, Penguin Books, 2003.

Jeffers, Susan. *Feel the Fear and Beyond: Dynamic Techniques for Doing It Anyway*, Ebury Press, 1999.

Jeffers, Susan. *Feel the Fear and Do It Anyway*, Ballantine, 1988.

Kassorla, Irene C. *Go for It*, Dell, 1985.

Koltnow, Emily. *Congratulations! You've Been Fired*, Ballantine, 1990.

Leider, Richard. *The Power of Purpose*, Berrett-Koehler, 2005.

Leider, Richard, and David Shapiro. *Repacking Your Bags—Lighten Your Load for the Rest of Your Life*, Berrett-Koehler, 1995.

Levoy, Gregg. *Callings Finding and Following an Authentic Life*, Three Rivers Press, 1998.

Linehan, Marsha. and Kelly Egan. *Asserting Yourself*, Facts on File, 1987.

Mallinger, Allan, M.D., and Dweyze, Jeannette. *Too Perfect: When Being in Control Gets Out of Control*, Ballantine, 1993.

Mayer, Jeffrey J. *If You Haven't Got the Time to Do It Right—When Will You Find the Time to Do It Over*, Fireside, 1991.

McGee-Cooper, Ann. *You Don't Have to Go Home from Work Exhausted! The Energy Engineering Approach*, Bowen & Rogers, 1990.

McKay, Matthew, and Fanning, Patrick. *Self-Esteem: A Proven Program of Cognitive Techniques for Assessing, Improving, and Maintaining Your Self-Esteem*, New Harbinger, 2000.

Morgenstern, Julie. *Organizing from the Inside Out: The Foolproof System for Organizing Your Home, Your Office and Your Life*, Owl Books, 2004.

Nash, Laura, and Howard Stevenson. *Just Enough Tools for Creating Success in Your Work and Life*, John Wiley & Sons, 2005.

Oldham, John. *Personality Self-Portrait*, Bantam, 1990.

Orlick, Terry, Ph.D. *Embracing Your Potential*, Human Kinetics, 1998.

Richardson, Cheryl. *Take Time for Your Life*, Broadway, 1999.

Seligman, Martin. *Learned Optimism: How to Change Your Mind and Your Life*, Pocket, 1992.

Schlossberg, Nancy. *Overwhelmed: Coping with Life's Ups and Downs*, Lexington Books, 1999.

Sher, Barbara, and Annie Gottlieb. *Teamworks: Building Support Groups That Guarantee Success*, Warner, 1991.

Simon, Sidney. *Getting Unstuck: Breaking through Your Barriers to Change*, Warner, 1989.

Sinetar, Marsha. *Living Happily Ever After: Creating Trust, Luck and Joy*, Villard, 1990.

Sinetar, Marsha. *Sometimes Enough Is Enough: Spiritual Comfort in a Material World*, HarperCollins, 2000.

Sinetar, Marsha. *To Build the Life You Want, Create the Work You Love*, St. Martin's Griffin,1995.

St. James, Elaine. *Simplify Your Life—100 Ways to Slow Down & Enjoy the Things That Really Matter*, Hyperion, 1994.

Stephan, Naomi. *Finding Your Life Mission: How to Unleash that Creative Power and Live with Intention*, Stillpoint, 1989.

Stoddard, Alexandra. *The Art of the Possible*, Collins, 1996.

Tannen, Deborah. *You Just Don't Understand: Women and Men in Conversation*, Harper, 2001.

Van Oech, Roger. *A Whack on the Side of the Head: How Can You Be More Creative*, Warner, 1998.

Viscott, David. *Risking*, Pocket, 1982.

Walker Betty, Ph.D., and Marilyn Mehr, Ph.D. *The Courage to Achieve: Why America's Brightest Women Struggle to Fulfill Their Promise*, Simon & Schuster, 1992.

Wegscheider-Cruse, Sharon. *Learning to Love Yourself*, HCI, 1981.

Whitmyer, Claude and Salli Rasberry. *Running a One-Person Business*, Ten Speed Press, 1994.

Winston, Stephanie. *Getting Organized*, Warner, 1991.

Zichy, Shoya. *Women and the Leadership Q: Revealing the Four Paths to Influence and Power*, McGraw-Hill, 2000.

Career-Related

Allen, David. *Getting Things Done: The Art of Stress-Free Productivity*, Penguin, 2002.

Anderson, Nancy. *Work with Passion: How to Do What You Love for a Living,* New World Library, 1995.

Armstrong, Howard. *High-Impact Telephone Networking for Job Hunters*, Adams Media Corp., 1992.

Barney, Robert. *Lifeboat Strategies: How to Keep Your Career Above Water During Tough Times*, iUniverse, 2000.

Beatty, Richard. *175 High-Impact Resumes*, Wiley, 2002.

Bloch, Deborah, and Lee Richmond. *Soul Work—Finding the Work You Love, Loving the Work You Have*, Davies-Black, 1998.

Boldt, Laurence G. *Zen and the Art of Making a Living—A Practical*

Guide to Creative Career Design, Penguin, 1999.

Bolles, Richard. *How to Create a Picture of Your Ideal Job or Next Career*, Ten Speed Press, 1989.

Bolles, Richard. *What Color Is Your Parachute?* Ten Speed Press, 2005.

Camden, Thomas, and Joan Mark. *How to Get a Job in the New York Metropolitan Area*, Surrey Books, 1993.

Brown, Robert E. and Dorothea Johnson. *The Power of Handshaking: For Peak Performance Worldwide*, Capital Books, 2004.

Cannon, Jan. *Now What Do I Do? The Woman's Guide to a New Career*, Capital Books, 2005.

Chin-Lee, Cynthia. *It's Who You Know: The Magic of Networking in Person and on the Internet*, Bookpartners, 1998.

Crowther, Karmen. *Researching Your Way to a Good Job*, Wiley, 1993.

Dilenschneider, Robert L. *50 Plus! Critical Career Decisions for the Rest of Your Life*, Citadel Press, 2004.

Elderkin, Kenton. *How to Get Interviews from Classified Job Ads*, Random House, 2005.

Figler, Howard. *The Complete Job Search Handbook*, Owl Books, 1999.

Gerber, Michael. *The E Myth Revisited: Why Most Small Businesses Don't Work and What to Do About It*, Collins, 1995.

Grappo, Joseph. *Top 10 Fears of Job Seekers: Your Guide to an Effective, Stress-Free Job Search*, Berkley Publishing Group, 1996.

Hansen, Katherine and Randall Hansen. *Dynamic Cover Letters*, Ten Speed Press, 2001.

Harrington, Mona. *Women Lawyers Rewriting the Rules*, Plume, 1995.

Hermann, Richard L., and Linda P. Sutherland. *The 110 Biggest Mistakes Job Hunters Make*, Federal Reports, 1992.

Ibarra, Herminia. *Working Identity: Unconventional Strategies for Reinventing Your Career*, Harvard Business School, 2004.

Jacobsen, Mary H. *Hand-Me-Down Dreams: How Families Influence Our Career Paths and How We Can Reclaim Them,* Three Rivers Press, 2000.

Jud, Brian and Charles Lipka. *Coping with Unemployment*, Marketing Directions, 1993.

Jukes, Jill, and Ruthan Rosenberg. *Surviving Your Partner's Job Loss*, National Press Book, 1993.

Justice, Peggy O'Connell. *Temp Track: Make One of the Hottest Job Trends of the 90's Work for You*, Petersons, 1993.

Kaye, Beverly, and Sharon, Jordan-Evans *Love 'Em or Lose 'Em: Getting Good People to Stay,* Berrett-Koehler, 2005.

King, Julie Adair, and Betsy Sheldon. *The Smart Woman's Guide to Interviewing & Salary Negotiation*, Thomson Delmar Learning, 1995.

King, Julie Adair, and Betsy Sheldon. *The Smart Woman's Guide to Resumes & Job Hunting*, Thomson Delmar Learning, 1995.

Krannich, Ronald. *Change Your Job Change Your Life*, Impact Publications, 2004.

Krannich, Ronald. *Salary Success—Know What Your Worth & Get It*, Impact Publications, 1990.

Krannich, Ronald and Caryl. *Dynamite Cover Letters*, Impact Publications, 1999.

Krannich, Caryl and Ronald. *Interview for Success: A Practical Guide to Increasing Job Interviews, Offers and Salaries*, Impact Publications, 2002.

Krannich, Ronald and Caryl. *The New Network Your Way to Job & Career Success*, Impact Publications, 1993.

Kennedy, Joyce Lain and Thomas J. Morrow. *Electronic Resume Revolution*, John Wiley & Sons, 1995.

Kroeger, Otto. *Type Talk at Work*, Delta, 2002.

Lauber, Daniel. *Nonprofits Job Finder*, Planning Communications, 2006.

Leeds, Dorothy. *Marketing Yourself: The Ultimate Job Seeker's Guide*, Perennial, 1992.

Levinson, Harry. *Career Mastery*, Berrett-Koehler, 1992.

Lonier, Terri. *Working Solo*, Wiley, 1998.

Mantis, Hilary Jane, and Kathleen Brady. *Jobs for Lawyers—Effective Techniques for Getting Hired*, Impact Publications, 1996.

McCarthy, Michael. *Mastering the Info Age*, Tarcher, 1990.

Medley, Anthony. *Sweaty Palms—The Neglected Art of Being Interviewed*, Warner Business Books, 2005.

Menchin, Robert. *New Work Opportunities for Older Americans*, iUniverse, 2000.

Miller, Susan D. *Be Heard the First Time: The Woman's Guide to Powerful Speaking*, Capital Books, 2006.

Moreau, Daniel. *Kiplinger's Survive & Profit from a Mid-Career Change*, Kiplinger Books, 1994.

Nierenberg, Andrea. *Million Dollar Networking: The Sure Way to Find, Grow and Keep Your Business*, Capital Books, 2005.

Nierenberg, Andrea. *Nonstop Networking: How to Improve Your Life, Luck and Career*, Capital Books, 2002.

Ormont, Ronda. *Career Solutions for Creative People,* Allworth Press, 2001.

Reck, Ross R., Ph.D. *The X-Factor: Getting Extraordinary Results from Ordinary People,* Wiley, 2001

Reich, Robert B. *The Future of Success,* Vintage, 2002.

Resnick, R. Linda, with Kerry H. Pechter. *A Big Splash in a Small Pond: Finding a Great Job in a Small Company,* Fireside, 1994.

Richardson, Bradley. *Jobsmarts for TwentySomethings,* Vintage, 1995.

Riehle, Kathleen A. *What Smart People Do When Losing Their Jobs,* John Wiley & Sons, 1991.

Roane, Susan. *How to Work a Room: The Ultimate Guide to Networking and Savvy Socializing,* Chrysalis Books, 2001.

Rogers, Natalie, H. *The New Talk Power: The Mind-Body Way to Speak Like a Pro,* Capital Books, 1999.

Roper, David H. *Getting the Job You Want Now,* Warner, 1994.

Sabah, Joe and Judy. *How to Get the Job You Really Want-And Get Employers to Call You,* Plume, 1992.

Sacharov, Al. *Offbeat Careers: The Directory of Unusual Work,* Ten Speed Press, 1988.

Sher, Barbara. *I Could Do Anything If I Only Knew What It Was,* Dell, 1995.

Sher, Barbara. *Wishcraft: How to Get What You Really Want,* Ballantine, 2003.

Sinetar, Marsha. *Do What You Love, The Money Will Follow,* Dell, 1989.

Stevens, Paul. *Expand Your Career Horizons—Stop Postponing the Rest of Your Life,* Ten Speed Press, 1993.

Stoodley, Martha. *Information Interviewing—What It Is and How to Use It in Your Career* Garrett Park Press, 1990.

Studner, Peter. *Super Job Search: The Complete Manual for Job Seekers & Career Changers,* Jamenair, 2003.

Tieger, Paul D. and Barbara Barron-Tieger, *Do What You Are: Discover the Perfect Career for You through the Secrets of Personality Type,* Little Brown, 2001.

Toropov, Brandon. *303 Off-the-Wall Ways to Get a Job,* Career Press, 1995.

Weinstein, Bob. *I'll Work for Free: A Short-Term Strategy with a Long-Term Payoff,* Owlet, 1994.

Wendleton, Kate. *Job Search Secrets,* Five O'Clock Books, 1996.

Wendleton, Kate. *Targeting the Job You Want,* Thomson Delmar Learning, 2000.

Williams, Mark A. *The 10 Lenses: Your Guide to Living & Working in a Multicultural World*, Capital Books, 2001.

Williams, Mark A. *Your Identity Zones: Who Am I? Who Are You? How Do We Get Along?* Capital Books, 2004.

Winter, Barbara. *Making a Living Without a Job—Winning Ways for Creating the Work You Love*, Bantam, 1993.

Yate, Martin. *Knock 'em Dead 2006: The Ultimate Job Seeker's Guide*, Adams Media Corp., 20th anniversary ed., 2005.

Yeager, Neil. *Career Map: Deciding What You Want, Getting It and Keeping It*, John Wiley & Sons, 1988.

INDEX